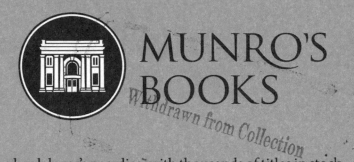

MUNRO'S BOOKS

Withdrawn from Collection

4/17
22.00

We're a book lover's paradise, with thousands of titles in stock. Browse the best in Canadian and international fiction, discover a new poet, or get lost in our extensive children's department.

A Victoria landmark, Munro's Books has been celebrating the pleasures of the printed word since 1963.

LET'S CELEBRATE!

Please join us on December 2nd as we celebrate the Canada issue of *Granta* magazine with Madeleine Thien and other special guests. Full details at **munrobooks.com**.

D0009862

1108 Government Street
Victoria, BC Canada
250-382-2464   munrobooks.com

GRANTA

12 Addison Avenue, London W11 4QR | email: editorial@granta.com
To subscribe go to granta.com, or call 020 8955 7011 (free phone 0500 004 033)
in the United Kingdom, 845-267-3031 (toll-free 866-438-6150) in the United States

ISSUE 141: AUTUMN 2017

GUEST EDITORS	Catherine Leroux, Madeleine Thien
DEPUTY EDITOR	Rosalind Porter
POETRY EDITOR	Rachael Allen
ONLINE EDITOR	Luke Neima
ASSISTANT EDITOR	Francisco Vilhena
SENIOR DESIGNER	Daniela Silva
EDITORIAL ASSISTANTS	Eleanor Chandler, Josie Mitchell
SUBSCRIPTIONS	David Robinson
PUBLICITY	Pru Rowlandson
TO ADVERTISE CONTACT	Kate Rochester, katerochester@granta.com
FINANCE	Morgan Graver
SALES AND MARKETING	Iain Chapple, Katie Hayward
IT MANAGER	Mark Williams
PRODUCTION ASSOCIATE	Sarah Wasley
PROOFS	Katherine Fry, Jessica Kelly, Lesley Levene, Sophie Marcotte, Vimbai Shire, Louise Tucker, Lindeth Vasey, Mandy Woods
CONTRIBUTING EDITORS	Daniel Alarcón, Anne Carson, Mohsin Hamid, Isabel Hilton, Michael Hofmann, A.M. Homes, Janet Malcolm, Adam Nicolson, Edmund White
PUBLISHER AND EDITOR	Sigrid Rausing

ANANSI PUBLISHES VERY GOOD BOOKS

INDEPENDENT CANADIAN PUBLISHING SINCE 1967
HOUSEOFANANSI.COM

HOUSE OF ANANSI PRESS ACKNOWLEDGES THE FINANCIAL SUPPORT OF THE OMDC BOOK FUND, AN INITIATIVE OF THE ONTARIO MEDIA DEVELOPMENT CORPORATION.

Tenth Anniversary 2017

The Cundill History Prize

 McGill

Celebrating its 10th anniversary in 2017, the international Cundill History Prize recognizes the best history writing in English.

"History — good, readable, evidence-based history — is part of the toolbox of democracy."

Margaret MacMillan
2017 Chair of Jury

Administered by McGill University, the prize generously rewards the leading historians of our time, with a grand prize of US$75,000, and the two 'Recognition of Excellence' prizes of US$10,000.

The eminent Canadian historian Margaret MacMillan is joined by the British-American historian and author Amanda Foreman, the award-winning Oxford Professor Roy Foster, the decorated Canadian journalist and author Jeffrey Simpson, and the Oxford Professor of Modern China Rana Mitter to judge the prize in its anniversary year.

The winner will be announced at the Cundill History Prize Gala on November 16, 2017 in Montreal.

www.cundillprize.com

THE PETER CUNDILL FOUNDATION

BURGUNDY
ASSET MANAGEMENT LTD.

Tenth Anniversary 2017

The Cundill History Prize

 McGill

Celebrating its 10th anniversary in 2017, the international Cundill History Prize recognizes the best history writing in English.

Administered by McGill University, the prize generously rewards the leading historians of our time, with a grand prize of US$75,000, and the two 'Recognition of Excellence' prizes of US$10,000.

The eminent Canadian historian Margaret MacMillan is joined by the British-American historian and author Amanda Foreman, the award-winning Oxford Professor Roy Foster, the decorated Canadian journalist and author Jeffrey Simpson, and the Oxford Professor of Modern China Rana Mitter to judge the prize in its anniversary year.

The winner will be announced at the Cundill History Prize Gala on November 16, 2017 in Montreal.

www.cundillprize.com

"History — good, readable, evidence-based history — is part of the toolbox of democracy."

Margaret MacMillan
2017 Chair of Jury

LIGHT Souvankham Thammavongsa

HOW YOU WERE BORN Kate Cayley

DUKE Sara Tilley

COACH
HOUSE
BOOKS

FICTION

NON-FICTION

POETRY

The very first work of fiction from
the best-selling author of *City on Fire*

GARTH RISK HALLBERG

A *GRANTA* 'BEST YOUNG AMERICAN NOVELIST'

A piercingly
beautiful
treasure box
of a novella
about two
families in the
suburbs, now in a
newly designed,
full-color edition.

"Hallberg has a
fine novelist's grace
and sensitivity."
—*KIRKUS REVIEWS*

KNOPF

A FIELD GUIDE *TO THE*
NORTH AMERICAN FAMILY

GARTH RISK HALLBERG

*An
Illustrated
Novella*

Best-selling author of
CITY ON FIRE

©Chris Eichler

A FIELD GUIDE *TO THE* NORTH AMERICAN FAMILY

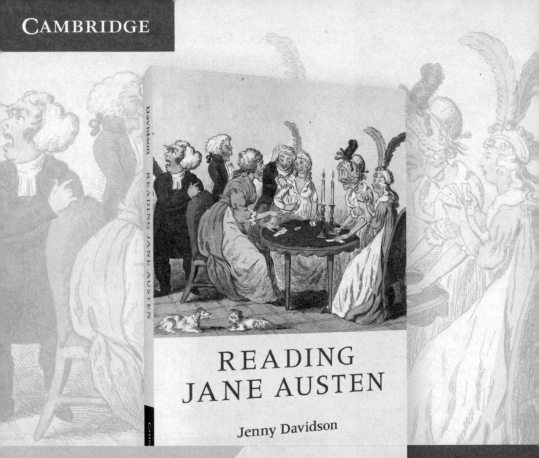

Creative
Writing
Online

- Fiction and poetry courses designed by UEA

- Beginner and intermediate level

- Delivered by experienced tutors

- Study anywhere at your own pace

- Supportive and friendly community

For more info on January 2018 courses visit
writerscentrenorwich.org.uk

University of East Anglia

WRITERS'
CENTRE
NORWICH

—— National Centre for Writing ——

New crime fiction course for January 2018!

AT THE OLD VIC

A CHRISTMAS CAROL

A NEW VERSION BY

JACK THORNE

RHYS IFANS

18 NOVEMBER 2017–20 JANUARY 2018

TICKETS FROM £12

PREVIEWS
PARTNER

OLDVICTHEATRE.COM

PRINCIPAL PARTNER

pwc

RBC

Royal Bank of Canada

THE FIRST WORD IN CANADIAN FICTION THE SCOTIABANK GILLER PRIZE 2017 SHORTLIST

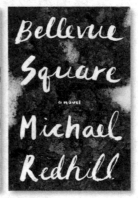

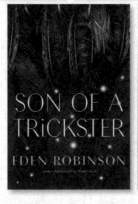

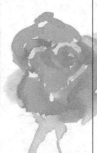

scotiabankgillerprize.ca

CONTENTS

Introduction

C'est fascinant de lire la liste des noms qui auraient pu être, tantôt très prosaïques (comme 'Efisga', acronyme de English, French, Irish, Scottish, German, Aboriginal), tantôt lyriques (comme 'Borealia', 'Vesperia', même 'Ursalia' qui signifie 'Terre des ours'). Une foule d'ursidés traversent d'ailleurs les textes qu'on nous a soumis. Encore aujourd'hui, l'ours règne sur notre imaginaire.

In 1867, Canada was carefully named a dominion, a designation borrowed from Psalm 72 of the Bible: 'He shall have dominion also from sea to sea, and from the river unto the ends of the Earth.' From the beginning – the name Canada was born from the Huron-Iroquois word *kanata* – dominion was linked to the land, languages and lives of Indigenous peoples.

The land has sixty unique Indigenous language dialects, and, according to census data, more than two hundred languages reported as a mother tongue or home language.

In the country's Northwest Territories, there are eleven official languages, including French, Tłıchǫ and Inuktitut. Canada attained full sovereignty from the British Parliament in 1982, but it is a 150-year-old nation state that has been peopled for at least 14,000 years.

Et qui est le théâtre d'entreprises coloniales depuis plus de 480 ans.

When we took on the task of guest-editing this issue of *Granta*, we opened the call for submissions as widely as we could. Our only parameter: *What is being imagined here, now?* Within a few weeks, we received over a thousand pieces of prose and poetry in French and English. We read everything. For months we floated at sea, trying to understand what had been gathered.

En mer, sur terre, sous terre, dans le désert, en banlieue, au ciel, prises dans les glaces, tapies dans la forêt . . .

'The white blood of language', écrivait France Daigle dans une version antérieure de son texte. Cinq mots qui disent tout sur ce fluide vital qui parfois nous échappe et nous laisse exsangues.

Et il n'y avait que Margaret Atwood pour ajouter à cette énumération les mots 'craton, molten blob of lava et *Amanita muscaria*'.

Language becomes its own landscape in this issue of *Granta*. Language falls apart, twists, reformulates, shatters and revives itself. Animal and self, unfinished history, land and waterways, colonization and dispossession, settlement and refuge – all these nouns are part of the truth of this place. Here, like everywhere, there will be no cohesive mythology, no finality to what can be seen; on the contrary, in reading these thousand pieces, I experienced a combative and polyphonic understanding of ourselves, a complexity that carries force. 'There was no inquiry,' writes Alex Leslie, 'because nobody knew where they were going or what was going to happen or how long it would take. It's a simple story.' Benoit Jutras gives thanks 'because the floor in my room hid a lagoon'. Naomi Fontaine, who lives between Innu-aimun and French, tells us, 'Language is a risk that a nation takes.'

We wanted more than we could include here; some pieces we dearly hoped would form the heart of this issue could not, in the end, be written or completed. I think this speaks to our charged historical moment, and to a nation state that is troubled by itself. Moreover, what unsettles the world must also unsettle Canada – a post-colonial country whose cities are among the most ethnically diverse on the planet, and where the rate of environmental change has pitched us all into unknown territory. We are a people who remember and forget simultaneously, slowly learning to share a land that persistently eludes a single language. ∎

Madeleine Thien

So true. As soon as you try to hold the word it changes form.

Il est difficile au Québec de prononcer le mot Canada sans éprouver le sentiment d'une certaine friction. Le mot est pourtant si rond, si lisse au toucher, comme un cube de glace. C'est d'ailleurs la perception que bien des francophones, surtout quand ils sont assis au cœur de la province, de ses discours et de ses événements, ont de la culture anglo-canadienne. C'est aussi le préjugé auquel j'ai adhéré à une certaine époque. Les grands espaces enneigés. Le silence. Le vent sur la plaine. Une littérature du gris et du non-dit. Aux antipodes de la fête orageuse née dans la marmite québécoise à la fin des années soixante.

Depuis, bien des auteurs canadiens-anglais ont fait vaciller mes idées reçues, mais rien n'aurait pu les anéantir avec plus de vigueur que l'expérience de plonger dans les quelque mille textes soumis à *Granta*. J'y ai découvert non seulement des forces éclatées et une nouvelle idée du sublime, mais surtout l'écho de cette friction qui habite chacun de mes regards sur ce pays. Les anglos (j'inclurai dans ce terme tous ceux qui choisissent de s'exprimer dans cette langue, toutes origines confondues) se sentent finalement aussi mal à l'aise, à l'étroit, dérangés à l'intérieur du concept du Canada que les francophones. Eux aussi poussent sur les parois de la sphère, eux aussi ragent, s'inquiètent, essaient, déplacent, planent, bandent et fracassent.

The divide – or union – between thought and feeling is imagined in remarkably different ways by both the French- and English-language writers. And maybe this is why, in translation to English, certain things (for instance verb tenses, poetics and the folding of time-space), seem to defy English even as they read ingeniously in English.

Parmi les textes français, ce sont les voix les plus discordantes que, sans les chercher, j'ai d'instinct voulu suivre; celles qui parlent depuis l'extérieur, depuis la marge, celles

I've been thinking
through two thoughts by
Nicholas Ostler: that a specific
language allows us 'to stand
on the shoulders of so much
ancestral thought and feeling'
and that 'to tell the story is not
always to understand it'.

qui érodent le centre immuable qu'on veut nous imposer pour y infiltrer rêve, colère et beauté. C'est dans cette abrasion, dans ces explorations, dans les rires jaunes et l'éclatement que je suis parvenue à sentir qu'il était bel et bien possible de dire quelque chose de vrai sur la littérature d'ici.

Cette sélection de textes se situe là où les langues, les passés, les blessures se rencontrent, là où la dissonance se fait révélation. Et ce carrefour recèle aussi une route invisible: celle qui mène à toutes les œuvres que nous n'avons pas pu inclure. Pour un auteur, être responsable du sort du travail des autres peut devenir un véritable supplice, sans doute parce que les fragilités, le courage et l'adresse qui surnagent ou se tapissent dans chaque texte nous demeurent toujours apparents. Nous aurions pu publier une dizaine de versions différentes de ce numéro de *Granta*. Je crois que ces absents continuent de résonner avec la même force que ceux que nous avons retenus. Ils retentissent et habitent le reste comme une idée fixe, une image en négatif. Comme les mots habitent le réel; comme les histoires habitent un pays. ∎

Krista Foss writes,
'What happened exactly? A
convergence of elements we
thought we understood: rain,
wind and snow'.

Catherine Leroux

All work in translation is available to read on Granta.com in the original French, as is this introduction in both languages.

ANDERSON BOY WALKS IN

TRANSPORTATION NORTH

"A TOUGH KID", said a Tuk resident, referring to Bemard Andreason's long walk over the barrens from Inuvik to Tuktoyaktuk. During the walk many bodies of water had to be crossed by the youth, who is pictured above resting after his ordeal in his home at Tuktoyaktuk. -- Photo by R. Gauthier

Search for three Stringer Hall students, missing since June 23rd, centered on the Tuktoyaktuk area Saturday July 8 after Bernard Andreason, 11 years old, was found walking the NCPC power line 8 miles south of the community.

The search for the missing youngsters immediately swung to the Tuk area with RCMP and residents of that community covering 40 miles of the pole line south without success. Twenty-four hours later Inuvik. The search continues for Dennis Dick, 13, third member of the party of youngsters who had attempted to walk the pole line to Tuktoyaktuk.

Bernard Andreason was sighted by an Eldorado Nuclear pilot flying between Tuk and Inuvik. He was immediately rescued by an IOL helicopter which delivered him to the Tuktoyaktuk Nursing Station where he was treated for exposure and kept overnight.

The search for the three boys which had been slowing down for want of new leads has concentrated the efforts of searchers from both Tuktoyaktuk and Inuvik on the NCPC power line. Young Andreason, on being found, advised his rescuers that he

LAWRENCE JACK ELANIK
(11 years old)

FOUND DEAD

had become separated from his two companions about two days previously.

Further investigation suggested that he had lost track of time and believed he had been away only a little over a week. It was further suggested that his two companions may have turned back and attempted to retrace their steps to Inuvik.

A medical estimate of the time of death of Jack Elanik was approximately a week

DENNIS DICK
(13 years)

STILL MISSING

prior to his being discovered.

At press time, searchers continue to examine the pole line area on the ground in 2-mile overlapping sections. The searches carried out over the preceding two weeks had included the NCPC power line with a number of aircraft flying the line between Inuvik and Tuktoyaktuk at low altitude since there was a possibility that the boys may have attempted to walk the line to Tuktoyaktuk.

Federal Transport Minister Don Jamieson, on July 4, announced 6 major proposals being considered to improve the economics of the western provinces and upgrade resource development in the forestry and mineral regions of the Yukon and B. C. Some of the proposals revealed by the Transport Minister directly affect the development of transportation services in the Mackenzie District of the NWT.

These are: (1) extension of the Liard highway to Fort Simpson, NWT. Extension of this highway from the BC-NWT boundary to Fort Simpson, NWT would provide direct access to motor vehicle traffic from the Alaska Highway at Fort Nelson to the Mackenzie Highway, which is being built by the Federal Government. It would line the entire Mackenzie Valley with the new rail head at Fort Nelson and the highway systems of southwestern Canada.

(2) The Skagway-Carcross Highway. Construction of this road would provide Whitehorse, Yukon and the southwestern corner of the Yukon with road access to the sea via Skagway, Alaska and would greatly benefit the economy of this area of the Yukon. The construction of the Dempster Highway presently being carried out by the federal government between Dawson City and Inuvik would permit goods destined for the western arctic to be carried by container from the deepsea port of Skagway *down to Mackenzie. Delta Center.*

(3) *BC-Yukon extension of existing railway lines. Such extension would provide raw railway transportation links from the Yukon to the Prince Rupert area at a greatly reduced rate. The railway would connect the Yellowknife gold fields to the Pacific port and provide direct rail service from the Yukon to support and distribute raw freight to the Great Slave lake area. The western arctic Yukon and western arctic transportation corridor.*

The time required to expand and upgrade the transportation services outlined above is 10 years.

'Bennett conned on oil pact'

Vancouver Province

Premier Bennett, by signing a memorandum of agreement today on joint pollution control efforts with Washington state, is thoughtlessly playing into the hands of the oil interests, provincial Liberal Leader David Anderson said Sunday.

The statement of intent to co-operate on handling oil spills and similar problems in Washington-B.C. waters will be signed this morning by Bennett and Gov. Dan Evans at the Blaine Peace Arch.

It is the result of joint nego-

tiations begun following an oil spill at the Atlantic Richfield oil refinery at Cherry Point, Wash., which leaked oil onto Washington and B.C. beaches.

Anderson is opposing in U.S. courts plans to ship Alaskan oil from a pipeline down the west coast. He said Bennett's decision to sign the agreement with Evans is "predicated on the assumption that we are going to lose the fight."

Evans has favored the refinery, he said, and has "conned the premier into believing

that by signing a piece of paper they will solve the problems."

"Bennett doesn't understand the distinction between agreeing to do something and what you do after signing the agreement."

The government should oppose the tanker plan rather than sign an agreement to work out joint plans for handling any resultant spills. But instead of protection, said Anderson, "the people are getting the game of politics."

"Bennett is playing into the hands of Americans who want the (Alaska oil) pipeline to go through."

Details of the memorandum of agreement have not been released.

Evans said last week he thinks Puget Sound can be preserved without banning tankers and the greatest danger is from ruptured fuel lines and small spills, rather than from larger spills from ocean tankers plying U.S. and Canadian waters.

LONG TRIP TO THE DUMP

Uniroyal's Toronto warehouse staff in Don Mills was a little mystified this week when it opened a crate that had been shipped collect from the NWT and found that it contained 575 pounds of scrap metal.

The crate hadn't been addressed to any particular department and had remained unclaimed for three weeks before it was finally searched. A check with all those involved uncovered the details of a 4800 mile journey to the dump.

Serveral months ago Uniroyal shipped the crate, which contained a 500 gallon inflatable rubber drum used to store fuel, to one of its western distributors who in turn supplied it to a customer doing exploration work 1500 miles from Yellowknife north of the 79th parallel. Arctic land use regulations set by the federal government dictate that all garbage must be burned and all noncombustible material

transportation company didn't send the old crate to the dump but noting the Uniroyal return address put it on a truck bound for Edmonton. From there it was delivered to Uniroyal's 895 Don Mills Road office with a collect freight bill for $104.02.

The transport company says they won't charge Uniroyal for assisting in maintaining the ecological balance in the Arctic and as soon as the company can dispose of the crate the world's longest trip to the dump will have ended.

Molstad

Replaces Flynn

Dave Flynn, former area administrator at Tuktoyaktuk, and most recently serving as Chief of the Development Division of the Local Government Department at Yellow-

FIRST in a series of new British nautical stamps of interest to Canadian collectors shows a coast guard in early 19th century uniform against the background of a stormy sea and a ship in distress.

NWT MEDICARE OFFICE MOVES NORTH

The territorial government's Medicare Plan Office has moved its office and 5 staff people from Edmonton to Yellowknife.

All NWT residents listed as eligible for Medicare services will be receiving a new registration card shortly, noting the relocation of the office in Yellowknife. A special notification has been made directly to hospitals and medical practitioners.

Page 3 of Inuvik newspaper the *Drum*, 13 July 1972
Courtesy of the author

MANGILALUK'S HIGHWAY

Nadim Roberts

Dennis spotted the cigarettes on their dorm supervisor's bed. He hesitated a moment, then stuffed the pack of Rothmans King Size into his shirt pocket. No one was around to witness the offence except his two best friends, Jack and Bernard. The rest of the boys in Stringer Hall, their residential school dormitory, were outside playing. Dennis, Jack and Bernard shot out the front doors and past the playground to find a quiet place to smoke. The warm Arctic sun, which would not set for a few more weeks, hovered in the sky above them as they passed around a cigarette.

It was 24 June 1972, a Saturday, and in a week the three boys and their classmates attending the Sir Alexander Mackenzie School in Inuvik would head home to their small hamlets across the Arctic for summer break. By seven o'clock that evening the boys were back in the dorm. Their supervisor, Annie, was in a rage. She demanded to know who had taken her cigarettes. Dennis eyed Bernard from the far end of the dorm. He looked frightened, and shook his head, signalling for Bernard not to say anything. Punishment at residential school could be severe, especially for stealing. But Bernard would never snitch on Dennis. The next morning, after chapel, Bernard overheard a few of his classmates telling Annie they knew who took her cigarettes. They'd been caught. Bernard ran to find Dennis and

Jack. He found them in Grollier Hall, the Roman Catholic dorm, and suggested they hide somewhere. They walked into the hills behind their school, sweating under the hot sun, until they found a pond. They waded into the cool, shallow water with their clothes on, splashing each other and laughing. Dennis still had the cigarettes in his shirt pocket. They were ruined now.

From the pond, the boys walked in the direction of the highest hill, where they could see power lines unspooling to the north-east. The 69,000-volt transmission lines had been strung the previous month. 'These lines go all the way to Tuk,' Dennis told his friends. He and Bernard were from Tuktoyaktuk, on the shores of the Arctic Ocean. If they followed the power lines, they'd be home in a few hours, Dennis said. School would be over soon anyway, and if they left now, they could avoid getting in trouble.

They took one last look down the other side of the hill towards Inuvik and began walking. Around them, delicate flowers bloomed among the moss, and sharp blades of grass scratched their ankles. They joked about how tough they'd be by the time they got home.

Dennis and Bernard were cousins who'd grown up together in Tuk. At thirteen, Dennis was squat, and still waiting on a growth spurt. Bernard, though only eleven, was taller, and had long limbs outgrowing his torso. His hair fell messily onto his forehead above long, almond-shaped eyes. Jack was from Sachs Harbour, a town on Banks Island, the westernmost island of the Arctic Archipelago. He was the smallest of the three, and prone to illness.

Hours later, the midnight sun was low on the horizon, reflecting off a glassy lake. Its glare was now soft, bathing the land in shades of magenta and gold. Ahead, Dennis saw a familiar formation. 'Look,' said Dennis. 'There's a pingo!' In front of them was a forty-foot-high conical hill that looked like the pingos that surround Tuk. Pingos are only found in a permafrost environment, and are the result of frozen ground being forced upwards by the pressure of subterranean water. For centuries, the Inuit of the Mackenzie Delta region have used them as navigational aids and lookouts for hunting. Visible from dozens of kilometres away across the tundra, they jut up against the northern horizon like mini volcanoes.

The boys raced towards the pingo.

But it was just another hill, one of many with no end in sight. Worn out, they looked for a place to sleep and found a log that would shield them from the chilly north-west winds. All they had on were T-shirts, shorts and sneakers. The day had been hot, but now they were shivering. They huddled closer to keep warm, and Bernard began to pray, as he did every night before bed at Stringer Hall.

'Our Father in heaven, hallowed be your name,' he whispered to the skies above. 'Lead us not into temptation, but deliver us from evil.'

Today, the only way to travel between Inuvik and Tuk in the summer months is by plane. In June 2017, forty-five years after Dennis, Jack and Bernard started walking home from residential school, I boarded a nineteen-seat white-and-blue DHC-6 Twin Otter. The 140-kilometre flight would take thirty minutes. From the air, the hummocky landscape resembled a camouflage pattern: greens and browns of all shades pockmarked with hundreds of lakes and waterways. What from high above appears to be solid grassland is anything but. The permafrost prevents water drainage, and after the spring thaw, the land above it becomes a bog of decomposing vegetation and moss that, like quicksand, can swallow animals as large as caribou.

During the winter months, an ice road capable of supporting cars, trucks and Skidoos along the frozen Mackenzie River, used to connect Inuvik and Tuk. But a month before my arrival, the ice road was closed for good by the Government of the Northwest Territories after decades of service. From the plane I could see occasional glimpses of a new, near-finished road. This was the long-awaited Inuvik–Tuk all-season highway that would open in a few months.

In 1959, the Canadian government decided to build a 730 kilometre gravel road from just east of Dawson City, Yukon, to Inuvik. Oil and gas exploration in the region was thriving and a highway across the Arctic Circle was needed to transport equipment and men to and from the drill sites. By 1972, Prime Minister Pierre Trudeau had announced the construction of yet another highway, between Fort Simpson and Inuvik, after which, he promised, work would begin on the final stretch of a highway that would connect Inuvik to Tuk. Trudeau compared the new roads to the famous routes pioneered by fur traders 150 years earlier. 'This road has been a dream until now,' he said.

It remained a dream for a long time. The final piece of the 'Roads to Resources Program', which would connect Inuvik to Tuk, and by extension Canada to the Arctic Ocean, immediately ran into problems. Oil and gas exploration waned, and the project was deemed too expensive and challenging. For half a century, the road remained a dormant hope.

Then, in 2010, Prime Minister Stephen Harper arrived in Tuk for a visit. Tuk's mayor Merven Gruben asked Harper for one thing, and one thing only. The highway, a legacy project that would link the country from coast to coast to coast and reduce the costs of petroleum exploration in the Beaufort Sea. Harper was convinced, and planning for a highway started the same day he flew back to Ottawa.

Upon landing in Tuk, I rode a cargo van into town. Driving down the town's main road, Beaufort Road, we passed small wood-frame homes resting only a few metres above the low peninsula that curves into Kugmallit Bay on the Arctic Ocean. The next day, I attended the hamlet's council meeting. The current mayor, Darrel Nasogaluak, and his fellow councillors eagerly discussed the $500,000 beautification project under way for the opening of the highway in November. In anticipation of all the tourists they hoped would now visit, workers were coating dozens of buildings in candy-like shades of paint they hoped would make the town unforgettable.

Since he'd become mayor, Nasogaluak's job had consisted largely of preparing Tuk for the opening of the new road. Beyond attracting tourists, he told me he hopes the road will renew interest in oil and gas drilling in the region. (Nasogaluak challenged Justin Trudeau's five-year Arctic drilling ban, telling the PM at a recent town hall meeting in Yellowknife, 'We're at a loss of what we'll do next.')

At 32 per cent, Tuk's unemployment rate is three times that of the rest of the Northwest Territories, and five times the Canadian average. For Nasogaluak, the road represents more than an all-weather route to their hamlet: it's a long-awaited path that he and many others in the town of 900 hope will help their community prosper.

In the coming months, the council will begin consulting on the name of the new highway. Merven Gruben's family wants the highway named after their recently deceased patriarch, Eddie Gruben. Eddie founded E. Gruben Transport, which was building the highway with Inuvik-based Northwind Industries. He was an influential figure in the Northwest Territories and died a multimillionaire at age ninety-six.

But another proposed name acknowledges a different part of Tuk's history. Many of the town's elders are residential school survivors. None of them have forgotten that day in June 1972 when three of their classmates ran away. Back when the road was still a dream, those boys attempted to walk it.

Dennis, Jack and Bernard woke up sore from their first night sleeping on the ground. They looked at the sun and guessed it was around noon. They were famished. They picked some cranberries and blackberries, and found an empty pop can that they filled with water from a stream. Away from the strict authority of Stringer Hall, they felt free. Once the staff at the residential school realized the three boys were missing, they launched a search. This was the fifth runaway attempt of the school year. The previous escapees had all been found. Helicopters scanned the land near Inuvik, and canoes searched the channels and lakes. Students conducted a house-to-house survey in town. No one imagined the boys would try to walk to Tuk.

The warm weather began to change. Squalls from the north-west brought the temperature down, and rain began to fall. The power lines reached a swift river, and the boys tried to cross it. When the water reached their necks, they got scared and turned back. They were soaked, and every gust of wind felt like a punishing lash. Jack was feeling ill, so they decided to find somewhere to sleep. Jack lay between Dennis and Bernard to keep warm, but he wouldn't stop crying. On the third day, the wind was still unrelenting and the sky darker. As they ate berries that morning, Jack begged Dennis and Bernard to return to Inuvik with him. Jack and Bernard turned back, but Dennis didn't follow. Bernard couldn't stop thinking about him. Bernard told Jack to wait for him as he went to talk some sense into Dennis. When he reached the river where he'd last seen him, he was gone. Bernard yelled his cousin's name, but only the wind howled back. He returned to Jack and they found some bushes that offered a little cover from the hard rain and slept.

Jack's crying woke Bernard up the next morning. Jack was too sick to find food. Bernard picked some berries and fetched water in the pop can. Jack had lost a lot of weight. Bernard knew they were in trouble and needed help, but didn't know if he should continue on to Inuvik, or head for Tuk, where he hoped Dennis might already be.

'I really want you to come with me,' Bernard said. But Jack wouldn't get up. Bernard told him that if he came to Tuk, they could slide down the big hill together in the wintertime, and that he could see the pingos. But Jack was too weak. 'Go without me,' he said. Bernard didn't want to leave him, but knew if they remained together, they would die together.

Tuk is a town founded by survivors. In 1902, contact with whalers led to a measles epidemic in Kitigaaryuit, an Inuit settlement at the mouth of the East Channel of the Mackenzie River. The dead in Kitigaaryuit outnumbered the living, who now considered the land cursed. A young man, Mangilaluk, went looking for a new place to live. He chose a location thirty kilometres away: Tuktoyaktuk, Inuvialuktun for 'it looks like a caribou'.

When Mangilaluk arrived at the place that would become Tuk, there was nothing on the peninsula but a few sod houses used for fishing in the summer. But it was an ideal site for a new start for his people, on the edge of a harbour and prime fishing ground for beluga and white fish. He started to build a permanent log house, and before long other families followed.

Mangilaluk served as chief, or Umialiq, for decades. Stories of his bravery, leadership and hunting skill persist today. People believed he was a shaman with the power to shape-shift into a polar bear. In July 1961, two decades after he died, Mangilaluk's granddaughter, Alice Felix, was eight months pregnant. While home alone one evening, she heard a knock on the door. She wasn't sure if she was awake or dreaming when the door swung open. A three-metre-tall polar bear stood in the doorway. It walked up to her, put its snowshoe-sized paw on her pregnant belly, and began to speak: 'If it's a boy, you name it after me.'

A traditional belief among the Inuit is that human spirits live on after death. After passing, the spirit of the deceased is able to inhabit the body of a newborn should the child receive the spirit's mortal name, whereupon the child acquires its namesake's soul and powers. When Alice gave birth to a son two weeks later, she gave him two names. The first was Mangilaluk. The second was Bernard.

Bernard felt guilty for leaving Jack behind. The weather was getting warmer, but the rains had created an unlimited supply of still water for mosquitoes to spawn in. A black cloud of them hovered around his face with a persistent buzz. When he reached the river where he'd last seen Dennis, he found a long stick to help him keep his balance as he crossed. The current was strong, but the cool water soothed the mosquito bites that covered his arms and legs. He inched his way across, the water soon covering his chest, and made it to the other side.

The ground was mossy and damp. His feet began to itch in his waterlogged sneakers. He desperately scratched his feet, but the itch never went away. Above him, an airplane appeared in the sky. It looked like the same one that had taken him to residential school in Inuvik. It might even be the plane he was supposed to be on to take him home at the end of the school year. He wondered what kind of life awaited him if he made it back to Tuk alive.

At residential school, Bernard had found some consistency in his life. Every night he had a warm bed to sleep in, and there was always food to eat the next day. His life at home in Tuk was less stable. Shortly after he was born, his mother became ill with tuberculosis and spent two years in isolation in an Edmonton hospital. Different families looked after him until David and Bessie Andreason finally adopted him. A family of means, with one of the biggest dog teams in town, they had adopted other children as well. The record player was always on in their prefabricated house, and Bessie, who loved to dance, would pick Bernard up and teach him how to waltz, his small feet resting on hers.

Then, when Bernard was six, David became sick after eating badly prepared beluga. After he died, Bessie began drinking heavily and gambling. The record player stopped spinning, and they never waltzed around the living room again. On weekends, adults would pour into their home to play bingo and blackjack and drink the home brew that Bessie concocted in their bathtub with molasses and yeast. Its sweet aroma filled the house while it cured.

Soon, Bessie started seeing a new man who didn't want Bernard around any more. Bernard began moving from house to house again, staying with different friends and relatives, and often sleeping outside. In the winter he would steal clothes and blankets to build small nests underneath houses where he could sleep. In 1969, the principal at the Mangilaluk School decided it would be better for Bernard to attend residential school than stay uncared for in Tuk.

Residential schools had existed in Canada since 1831, but it wasn't until the 1950s that a significant number of them operated in the north. These government-sponsored religious schools were established to assimilate Indigenous children into Euro-Canadian culture by ripping them away from their families and communities. When Western European colonization and evangelization finally arrived in the Arctic, what had been a relatively unscathed Inuit culture began to change rapidly. Bernard's biological parents had been part of the first generation of Inuit that passed through these schools. Before 1955, fewer than 15 per cent of school-aged Inuit were enrolled in residential schools. Most children still lived on the land with their families, learning traditional skills and knowledge. Rather than teaching students how to hunt, skin game and build igloos and kayaks, residential schools taught a curriculum used for white children in Alberta.

By 1964, more than 75 per cent of Inuit children attended residential schools. Their values, language and customs were supplanted overnight by a culture that saw itself as benevolent and superior, and saw the Inuit as primitive beings in need of sophistication. The young Inuit who went through the residential school system experienced an assault on their traditional identities that had shattering consequences: they are often referred to as the 'lost generation'.

When Bernard arrived at Stringer Hall in Inuvik, he stared in awe. He'd never seen a two-storey building before. The school was split along religious lines. Anglican students stayed in Stringer Hall, and Catholic students in Grollier Hall. The identical dormitories, which rested on piles driven deep into the permafrost, were each meant to house 250 students, though they were often crammed with more.

Leonard Holman, a stout reverend with a thick grey moustache, gave Bernard the number his supervisors would know him by from then on: 356. His long black hair was shorn and replaced with a buzz cut. He took his first shower and then Holman showed him to his bed in A dorm. 'You're gonna be okay here,' he said.

Next door at Grollier Hall, things were not okay. Across the hall from the senior boys dormitory lived Paul Leroux, a young dorm supervisor from Granby, Quebec. He was involved in all manner of school life, from coaching soccer to taking photographs for the school yearbook. Some nights, he would invite boys into his room, where he gave them alcohol and showed them pornography. Once they were drunk, he encouraged them to perform sexual acts on each other, and then on him.

Leroux was one of four staff members to use Grollier Hall as a hunting ground for young boys. Over a span of twenty years, these four men would molest dozens of children and youths, spurring a cycle of abuse that would spread like a malignant cancer across the entire school, and follow many of the children back to their home communities. The year before Bernard ran away from Stringer Hall, he too was drawn into this tempest of sexual violence. The older brother of a friend, a senior boy in Grollier Hall, molested Bernard.

The Inuit tell stories of creatures called Ijiraat, elusive land spirits that can transform into any Arctic animal, or even into humans. They lie in wait for lone travellers, changing shape to trick them, so they can get close. They create mirages: when they are near, mountains or hills far in the distance appear to be much closer. After an encounter with Ijiraat, travellers experience memory loss and become disorientated.

A week had passed since Bernard left Inuvik, but he was losing track of time. When the sun doesn't set, it can feel as though time has stopped altogether. Its warmth felt good on his skin, but the heat brought the mosquitoes back. There was little skin left now for them to puncture. He was losing a lot of weight, and his pants kept sagging lower and lower on his diminishing frame.

Malnourished and exhausted from the dozens of kilometres he had already travelled, Bernard began hallucinating. He could no longer tell if he was awake or dreaming. He questioned whether he was still even alive. Sometimes when he was walking in this state, he could hear people ahead of him telling him to 'hurry up'.

He saw a pile of small bird bones. The thought that he too could end up an anonymous stack of bones on the land terrified him. For the first time since leaving Inuvik, he started to cry. He thought about Dennis and Jack, whom he had not seen for many days.

That night, he cried himself to sleep and had a nightmare. Large groups of people were walking from Tuk to Inuvik. Bernard was trying to catch up with them. He stopped a woman and asked if his mom, Bessie, was okay. 'She's okay,' she replied. 'She's waiting for you.'

While walking the next day, he'd hear voices calling out to him, but before he could reach them he'd realize he had strayed from the lines. Then he saw two women he recognized from Tuk. He pumped his tired legs as fast as he could, yelling as he ran, his heart pounding through his chest. They raised their heads and looked at him in puzzlement. They were reindeer.

Ahead of him, Bernard could hear a river. It was much bigger than the previous one, ninety-feet wide with thundering rapids. He started to cross, making an effort to be careful, but he lost his footing. He struggled against the current, trying to swim back to shore. He felt too weak to go on. If he allowed the river to swallow him, it would be over. He wouldn't need to fight any more.

O utside the Northern Store, one of Tuk's two stores, I met Gerry Kisoun, a member of the search team that looked for the boys. He remembers the gloom that fell over town when Jack Elanik was discovered. He had been dead a week before his body was found, crawling with maggots and insects.

On 21 June, I attended Tuk's celebration for National Aboriginal Day. Dozens of families gathered by an outdoor stage where they ate caribou meat and drank tea that brewed on an open fire. A band played folk music, and a few adults and children jigged on the wooden stage. A woman named Marjorie who had attended Stringer Hall approached me and said that I should go and visit St John's Anglican Church and look for a Bible.

The door of the log church groaned loudly as I pushed it open. There were no longer any clergy tending to it. I passed by rows of empty benches on my way to the pulpit, then I opened the dusty maroon-coloured Bible that sat on it. On the first page was a dedication. 'Presented to St John's Mission Tuktoyaktuk,' it read. 'In memory of Dennis Dick.'

A couple days later, I visited Jasper Andreason, the biological brother of Dennis, and adoptive brother of Bernard. Like Bernard, he was adopted by Bessie and David Andreason as a boy. During those two weeks in June 1972, he had two younger brothers missing on the land. Of his eight biological siblings, Jasper is one of the few to have survived into old age. His sister Millie overdosed in a hotel on Vancouver's Downtown Eastside. Ruth ran into oncoming traffic and was killed in Edmonton. Albert was diagnosed with Aids. When he became sick with pneumonia, he hanged himself. 'They all came home in caskets,' Jasper told me.

The current pulled Bernard downstream. He had no energy left. Nearly two weeks had passed since he had walked away from Inuvik, and he had used every bit of his strength to get this far. He thought about his family back home: his stepmother, Bessie; his biological parents, Alice and Joseph; and his many siblings. He wanted to see them again. He kicked his feet and swung his arms to get back to the shore.

But he still had to cross this river. He climbed a hill to get a better view and saw a spot where he could safely cross. He traversed there and then came to two big lakes. Going around them would take too long, so he waded between them. The water was shallow, and he could see small fish darting between his legs. After passing through the lakes, he looked in the direction of Tuk. The sun was low and he was exhausted. He found a small hole to sleep in – it was a perfect fit for his emaciated body. He said his prayers, and fell asleep.

The next morning, a loud whirring noise woke him up. He thought he was dreaming, but he could feel the vibrations in the ground. He climbed out of the hole, and saw a helicopter getting ready to take off. He ran towards it, but it was too late. It was climbing higher and higher into the sky. Bernard was near Kitigaaryuit, the cursed land his great-grandfather and namesake Mangilaluk had left behind. Seventy years earlier, hundreds of his ancestors had perished here. Now, as Bernard crossed the landscape in which his descendants were buried, he felt his own death was near.

After walking for another hour, starving and barely able to keep his head up, he reached the top of a small hill. A sudden jolt brought life back into his weakened body: in the distance, he could see the pingos. This time they were unmistakable. He fell to the ground and started crying. He thought about Dennis and Jack, and wished they were with him. He hoped they were okay. Tears streamed down his face as he began to walk the last ten kilometres home.

A few days later, and a couple weeks before his twelfth birthday, Bernard was recovering in Inuvik General Hospital. After fourteen days of walking, he had lost nearly thirty pounds, and his shoes had to be cut off with scissors because his feet were so badly swollen. He was suffering from trench foot.

After Bernard was found, fifteen men in Inuvik and twelve in Tuk searched along the power lines for Dennis and Jack. Some walked for over sixteen hours, but they recovered only one body: Jack's. People figured Dennis either drowned or was eaten by an animal. Every summer his mother went looking for him along the power lines. She never found him.

The story of Bernard's mystifying survival soon spread across the Western Arctic. Tuk's mayor at the time, Emmanuel Felix, held a meeting with several other town elders after Bernard was found. They decided that should a highway ever be completed between Inuvik and Tuk, it should be named after the surviving boy. They insisted his Inuvialuit name should be used, the name of his great-grandfather and the founder of Tuk: Mangilaluk.

Bernard wasn't allowed back at residential school after he ran away, so he stayed in Tuk, occasionally attending the Mangilaluk School. Bernard's biological family took him back in. After years with the Andreasons, and then at residential school, it was tough to readjust to life with his biological family. For years, he couldn't bring himself to call his biological father 'Dad'.

In the years he had been away, his biological parents had started drinking more frequently. His mother beat him often, and life at home became unbearable for Bernard. He tried running away, but in a town cut off from the world, there was nowhere to run to.

Every year suicides increased in Tuk, and Bernard watched as fellow classmates from residential school were buried in the cemetery. Between September 1982 and October 1983, there were fifteen suicides, most of them boys and young men. Bernard's own sister attempted suicide. It was a wake-up call for his parents. They stopped drinking, but life never got much easier.

After Imperial Oil's 1970 discovery, a sudden windfall of money poured into Tuk. Young people left school to work temporary jobs in the oil industry. Tuk was a dry town, but bootleggers brought in an unlimited supply of alcohol they sold at four to five times what it cost in a store.

Tuk's two social workers couldn't keep up with the volume of work, which increased whenever the oil industry shut down for the season and people were left unemployed. The three largest oil companies in the region, Dome Petroleum, Esso Resources and Gulf Canada, were now offering alcohol and money counselling to their workers. But Tuk's own alcohol and drug abuse centre was forced to close its doors after its power bills went unpaid.

Bernard's older siblings knew there was something different about him. They beat him, trying to 'toughen him up', and 'make a man of him'. As he grew older, people in town began questioning him: 'Why aren't you married? Why aren't you with a girl?' Men in Tuk were expected to be hunters and trappers, and to have lots of kids. Bernard tried having relationships with women, but he could no longer hide who he was. One night a group of friends came into the house looking to party. Instead, they found Bernard and another man in bed.

Bernard began to drink to escape the depression and remoteness he felt as a gay man in the north. He drank to forget the physical abuse he suffered at the hands of his mother and older siblings, and he drank to forget the sexual abuse he endured as an eleven-year-old at residential school. Most of the time the drinking only made him numb. But sometimes it made him angry.

At 2 a.m. on 4 June 1982, while it was still light outside, Bernard entered the home of his next-door neighbours. Richard and Winnie were in bed sleeping. Bernard picked up their still-full coffee pot and smashed it on a wooden table, staining the carpet with coffee. Then he picked up their TV and threw it hard against the ground. Richard woke up and got out of bed to see what was going on. When he saw the mess Bernard was making, he told him to get out. Bernard closed his fist tightly and punched Richard above his right eye.

Richard fell to the ground, knocked out from the blow. Bernard lifted his boot and kicked him twice in the head. Then he found a log near the fireplace, picked it up and cracked it over Richard's skull. While blood from the deep lacerations on Richard's head spilled onto the carpet, Bernard tipped a washing machine over onto his still body. Then he went into the bedroom, where Winnie was still asleep. Bernard began punching her in the face.

The next day Bernard woke up in jail without any memory of the previous night. He was twenty-one years old and facing five years in prison for assault. During the trial a year later, his lawyer argued that Bernard was trying to turn his life around.

'I think that anyone who gets drunk and goes into an older couple's house and beats them brutally as you did can expect to go to jail for a longer time, a much, much longer time,' the judge said during his sentencing. 'So you are very fortunate.' Bernard got off easy: four months in prison at South Mackenzie Correctional Centre and two years' probation.

When he left prison, Bernard came back to Tuk and learned that his adoptive mom Bessie was ill. She was only sixty-seven, but years of excessive drinking had taken a toll on her. As she lay in a bed in the nursing station, Bernard called a minister to come and pray for her. The minister denied his request. Bessie was a drinker and a gambler, he said, and he wouldn't be praying for her. Instead, Bernard held his dying mother in his arms and prayed to a God that he hardly believed in any more.

After Bessie died, Bernard's determination to leave Tuk was solidified. He saw a newspaper ad about an Indigenous journalism programme at the University of Western Ontario in London. If he could write, he could share his story, and explain why he so desperately needed to leave Tuk. He booked his flights, packed his bags and planned never to return.

One evening in Tuk, I met with Bernard's younger brother, Stanley. He and his wife picked me up in their silver truck and we drove around town together. Stanley parked the car near a bench with a view of the bay. It was late at night, but the sun still shone like it was midday.

Stanley feels like he was spared, because he never attended residential school. But when his childhood friends returned from school in Inuvik, they brought the problems of residential school with them. Within the hierarchical society of residential school, kids learned to draw lines between themselves and others. It was Catholics vs Anglicans, abusers vs the weak, and any dispute was resolved with violence. 'Years ago,' he said, 'survivors started talking about sexual abuse, and they came back with that, too.'

In 1996, the Royal Canadian Mounted Police received a complaint from a former student at Grollier Hall who said a staff member sexually abused him. Mounties interviewed more than 400 former students of the school. Eight months into the inquiry, police had collected enough evidence to convince a judge to issue a search warrant for an apartment in Vancouver. It belonged to Paul Leroux.

The interviews with the students, now grown men, also produced evidence against two other former school employees, Joseph Jean-Louis Comeau and Jerzy George Maczynski. They all pled guilty. (A fourth school employee, Martin Houston, had been charged and convicted in 1962 for the sexual abuse of five boys at Grollier Hall.) During Leroux's trial in Inuvik he was fitted with a bulletproof vest. No one tried to kill him, but four of his former victims committed suicide during the trial.

An RCMP report revealed that sixty-one former residents of the school from the 60s and 70s had since died. Sixteen committed suicide, five died as a result of acts of violence, and three froze to death after heavy drinking. Fourteen died of natural or unknown causes. In 2002, the federal and territorial governments, along with the Roman Catholic Diocese of Mackenzie–Fort Smith, reached a historic out-of-court settlement with twenty-eight of twenty-nine Grollier Hall victims.

Stanley told me he understood why Bernard had to leave and never return. He wouldn't survive in a town like Tuk. He remembered a few nights before Bernard left, how badly he wanted to stay. 'I think he was more afraid to stay and live the way he was than he was afraid of leaving.'

In 1993, Bernard sat in a doctor's office in London, Ontario, to have his blood drawn. He was thirty-two, and had been in and out of treatment centres for alcoholism. The current rehab centre he was in required blood to test for hepatitis and other diseases. Bernard had hoped that when he left the north he might leave his problems behind. They followed him.

When Bernard came in for his results, the doctor wouldn't come near him. 'I have some good news and some bad news,' the doctor said, standing five feet away. 'What would you like to hear first?' Bernard asked for the bad news first. 'The bad news is you're HIV-positive.'

'What's that?' he asked. The doctor told him it was a virus that was going to develop into Aids. 'How long do I have to live?' Bernard asked.

'The good news is: if you take care of yourself, and that's a big if,' the doctor said, 'you might be able to live another ten years.' For the second time, Bernard felt his life being cut short. He didn't want to die.

After the diagnosis, Bernard was afraid to go near anyone. He stopped shaking people's hands and sat as far away from others as possible. He began to isolate himself. When Bernard switched on the TV, he saw stories about Aids on the news. In cities like New York and San Francisco, they were calling it 'gay cancer'. He saw Dr Peter Jepson-Young, a young Vancouver doctor, speaking about his own experience with Aids on TV. In Vancouver, there were more options for treatment, so he cashed his welfare cheque to buy a bus ticket.

In Vancouver, an HIV/Aids epidemic affecting thousands was prompting a public outcry. Doctors in the city were diagnosing two new HIV cases every day, and by 1997 approximately one person was dying each day. Bernard's weight started dropping, and he was tired a lot of the time. If he caught a cold, or felt a scratch or lump in his throat, he wondered if that was how he would die. He was scared to sleep because he thought he might not wake up the next day.

He began hearing about First Nations support groups for those with HIV and Aids. He started to meet other young Indigenous men and women in similar circumstances. Some were gay, and had been kicked out of their homes or shunned until they left their reserves. Others were drug users who felt they couldn't return to families and communities that were afraid to hug them or share the same cup. Many of his new friends died within a year of being diagnosed.

By 1995, doctors were experimenting with the Aids Cocktail, an antiretroviral therapy. Bernard was a perfect candidate for this new treatment. His appetite slowly came back. His viral loads decreased, and his CD4 and T-cell counts increased. When he hopped on the scale, his weight read 165: the weight before his diagnosis.

He moved to Prince George, where he helped form a group called the Frontline Warriors, which provides support, awareness education and prevention services to people living with Aids. By 2000, as many as one in four new HIV/Aids infections in Canada was among Indigenous people. Within this community there was poor access to testing and widespread discrimination on reserves against those infected. Bernard was concerned about how the younger generation of Indigenous men and women with HIV would fare. He began sharing his story of living with HIV on reserves and in high schools.

By 2008, Bernard, along with 80,000 other residential school survivors across Canada, began detailing their experiences in court-ordered private hearings to receive compensation. The more abuse an individual was subjected to, the more compensation they'd receive from the federal government. Bernard was too scared to tell a stranger about the sexual abuse he had suffered as a child, and withheld this information. For this reason, he received a smaller settlement. His suffering was deemed to be worth $40,000.

In August 2017, I met Bernard outside the Dr Peter Centre, a 30,000-square-foot healthcare facility that specializes in care for people living with HIV/Aids. It's named after Dr Peter Jepson-Young, the young Vancouver physician diagnosed with Aids that Bernard saw on television when he himself was first diagnosed.

We were meeting a few weeks after Bernard's fifty-sixth birthday.

His birthday comes two weeks after the day he survived the journey from Inuvik to Tuk, and since he turned twelve it has always been a reminder of the years he has lived since then, and of the years that were taken from Dennis and Jack.

As we walked through the halls of the Dr Peter Center, Bernard spotted a hanging quilt, imprinted with his photograph and those of other members of the centre. It was made fifteen years ago, at a time in Bernard's life where he said he had had 'enough of this dying crap'. In the photo he is smiling boyishly, crinkling his eyes. Not all the individuals with their photos on the quilt have lived as long as Bernard.

The phrase 'long-term survivor' refers to people who have been living with HIV since before the life-saving Aids Cocktail turned HIV into a manageable illness rather than a death sentence. Being a long-term survivor of HIV is associated with survivor's guilt: the mental trauma that occurs when a person believes he or she has done something wrong by surviving an event that others did not. Bernard, a long-term survivor, has witnessed countless friends lose their lives to Aids.

He often asks himself, 'Why me? Why did I survive?' It was the same question he asked himself as an eleven-year-old boy when he made it back to Tuk. Not a day of his life has gone by that Bernard has not thought about the two weeks he spent walking between Inuvik and Tuk. That journey is etched into his memory, and his dreams, where he still sees Dennis and Jack. The chronic guilt of survival has followed Bernard for forty-five years.

In Tuk, many people have already started unofficially calling the road between Inuvik and Tuk 'Bernard's Highway'. (One resident in town is suggesting they commemorate the boys by naming it the 'Freedom Trail'.) When the highway finally opens, Bernard wants to go back for his first visit in many years. He hopes to drive along the highway above the permafrost through the lakes and valleys he walked so long ago. When he sees the pingos in the distance, he will know that he is home. ∎

Benoit Jutras

Golgotha

Nassau

man covered by a wool blanket. sits on the ground. under a series of nails. pitchforks. spades. soiled pants. suspended in space.

I do not want to be heard, I want to be rasped, with shard-studded sleeves, jute and horsehair, to be deaf down to my sphincters so that my thing hanging down head first be hell for whoever goes there scattered, babe-battling tongue to tongue, subject-verb-saint-petroleum plastering my club-footed face to burn the books that stink of sage. I want to see my answer to every question bleed on a public totem for gnawing, a puddle on the ground wider than a gaol, my sixty-six nebulae afloat in it, so that the tablets of medicine and power may rise before you and silence the testaments. So the ashes may sing in *a* and *b* minor, so ketamine can taint the blood of Scottish lambs, turn into a discourse that chokes, thins out, sections, so that we lap it all up because drama, salvation, confession must. But truth means no, I want the remains, manure operating, ash trees growing through truncated fingers, I speak of lives in the mouth, flying masonry, I wish for the ram to digest the heart. From bed to world, an epistle is being written level with the petrol beneath joy and without me and it shames itself from mark to mark in a hunting shed. So that it is said: all the anniversaries of the idiot in bloom are mine now, and if I am ugly in a simple man's robes, it is so that I may become a stag and sleep on my hooves in Ovid's eleventh elegy.

Chorus

Our nation is a spell of nerves and gas. We say yes to monsters, to elegies etched in our palms. Summer comes in the guise of a mauve face, the ceaseless chewing on multiples of everything, our voices flaring up like lion's wine. We hide our pity in accounting books and the palest of excrements. Beneath our ribs, we are Aeschylus, Hesiod, Pindar. We are erecting the star of loss.

Jelinek

nude eyeless mouthless man. standing in space. over a tub. dense vapour. voice-over.

To the great sex- and act-cleansing storm; to the alphabetic woman who is taller than I; to take all and leave nothing; because my coliseum will be built of winters; to impossible definitions and silent cinema; to the fireflies penetrating our pores; to the science of the poor; to particles of sulphur on the uvula; to grease, unpunctuated nights, animal apparitions; because I see seats of water in all eyes; to the fear of becoming my mother; because music as carafe and suffocation; to the arithmetic man stronger than I; to tenderness as unction; because my machine flies twenty feet under houses; to my daughter and son turned into wars; to Laika's eyes on the Moon; for the sheep's succour in the park; for average things; for philosophy in trees; for the fish that fight mankind; to give me flour, water, darkness; because of the vertical force of strangers; for not speaking a word to me; for love in a Turin kitchen; because summer is a martial chorus; for my arms that are longer than the lists of history; for the olive oil in my hair on the shores of the Hudson River; for things undone and repaired by the morning's rules; because the floor in my room hid a lagoon; to negative hands; and to appease my ancient laughter and rights; to the warmth of the monkey holding on to my neck; because of ache acquired as a trade; to the talons of the barn owl; to that Greek winter, that Turkish winter; to night from the seventh of February to the second of June; to the Earth's shadow on my tabletop; to shame come on naked feet, thank you.

Chorus

Our ailment makes light of books. We sleep in fountains and child fists. Our loves are made of bent metal, of stolen rations. We refuse the whites of our pupils. We advance on our knees through the flesh, we throw bricks through the flesh. Crystal, mountain, mother: every day we turn into simple sorceries. To our shadows grown gigantic, we offer the water of our bodies. We speak to be left alone.

Translated from the French by Daniel Canty

Dorothea, 2001

THE REMEMBERER

Johanna Skibsrud

The Archive was indefensible and security breaches were at an all-time high when a girl (six years old, and in every other respect quite ordinary – living with her extended family somewhere in the banlieues) was discovered with what could only be described as a 'virtually limitless' power of recall. With 200,000 years of accumulated knowledge at stake, there seemed no better solution than to rely, once again, upon the faculties of the human mind.

Of course, they had to admit from the outset the idea was flawed. That it was, at best, a 'temporary measure'. But it was generally agreed – even by those scientists, historians, administrators and policymakers who (all bent on arriving, respectively, at a more sustainable solution) did not generally agree upon anything – that *if* properly educated, this remarkable young girl might buy them all a little valuable time.

A rigorous and fully funded education programme was quickly provided by the state, employing a team of researchers from every imaginable field. The 'Masters', as the team of thirty-seven came to be known, instructed the girl in every stage of the development of human thought covering every topic, every method, every (often conflicting) angle and approach to science, art, technology, trade and history itself over the past 200,000 years. The girl's appetite for knowledge proved so voracious that by the time she was nine years old her 'memory' extended back to the beginnings of human life on Earth. By eleven, she could remember rising from the mud; by twelve – with a reflexive shudder – the moment the first unicellular structure divided into two; by fourteen (and in not only accurate but moving detail) she could describe the conflicting pressures of gravity and time that caused the Earth to strain and shift, that set the continents adrift and gave birth to mountain ranges, ocean beds, polar ice and magnetic fields.

The fact that the girl was – aside from her extraordinary memory – really quite ordinary was not at first considered a disadvantage. She'd been removed from her extended family shortly after her genius was discovered – her only influences the thirty-seven Masters – but throughout she continued to demonstrate the usual range of human emotion, both delighting and confounding her Masters with bursts of frank affection, unreasonable anger and unexplained joy.

The programme had been named Whirlwind III after the first real-time computer system to benefit from the invention of core memory, but not only (the Masters boasted) did the girl already possess more core memory than any computer operating system that had been designed, she was also adaptable, fiercely loyal and unusually empathetic – three things still lacking from every other system of record-keeping, including the most advanced forms of AI.

As the girl grew older, however, her passions became less predictable, as well as less easy to temper. During an especially volatile moment at age fourteen, she even threatened to end her own life. ('What do I care?' she shrieked at the Masters. 'They're *your* memories – not mine!') The Masters did what they could to hush up the incident, but, inevitably, word got out – and the backlash was fierce. Up until this point, the programme had received wide and popular support; millions had happily followed the education and development of the bright-eyed, red-cheeked 'Rememberer' in the tabloids and the weekly news, but now nearly everyone began to complain. It was obvious (many early critics of the programme warned) that the burden of 200,000 years of accumulated knowledge was too much for any human being. It was *inhumane* – another especially vocal group argued – to invest 'the full range of human experience' in a single child precisely because it prevented her *from actually participating in* 'the full range of human experience'. No wonder the girl was increasingly troubled by insomnia and alternated between fits of rage and despair! No wonder that she had threatened to end her own life – and with it every possibility of establishing a more permanent record! No wonder that – shortly after, when she turned sixteen – she began to suffer from brief, inexplicable flashes of 'darkness'! (Petit mal seizures, the neurologists called them – but, upon further examination, no physical or biochemical cause could be found for the episodes and it was concluded that 'nothing' was wrong.)

The Masters fought among themselves, each one blaming another for the girl's emotional volatility and her 'absences', which (despite the doctors' prognosis) continued with increasing frequency. Each time they occurred – without explanation or warning – the girl would be unable to speak and, for several terrifying seconds, her face would go blank. Each time, 200,000 years of accumulated knowledge would flash horribly before the Masters' eyes.

And it was no wonder. Ten years had passed since the programme began, but still those (scientists, historians, administrators and policymakers alike) dedicated to arriving at a more permanent solution were no closer to finding one. The girl remained their only hope . . . and yet the situation was hopeless. The public still spoke out from time to time, but as they began to lose interest, it was the girl herself who became the programme's toughest critic – describing its limitations as 'insurmountable' and 'systemic', uniquely tied not only to the limits and vagaries of her education, but also to her own mind.

What should trouble them most, she protested, was that she was unable to pinpoint where one memory left off from another – or where they began. Rather than a continuous, chronological archive, her memories were instead fragmented, scattered, often vague. They would surface strangely, like photographs in a chemical bath – transformed into negative images of themselves. But rather than – like a photograph – indexing any actual experience, they seemed instead to mark a void.

And what (she demanded one day – chin jutted, eyes sharp and hard; the very 'picture' of adolescent impudence) of memories that could not be indexed at all? That were instead mere whiffs of sensations, brief bursts of colour, a feeling of being pricked by something – of 'going under', as beneath a sudden wave? What *in fact* were those memories, or any others (in which, say, she scoured the depths of the first oceans, or awakened in the mind of a cephalopod as the simple contrast between darkness and light), if not the products of someone else's imagination? What she 'remembered' was in any case not *knowledge*. It was speculation, conjecture . . . It was the purest of fictions!

In other moods, she would grumble that she 'hardly saw the point'. The history of human thought, she would sigh despairingly, was nothing more, after all, than an arduous dream. In still other moods, she would become fierce, aloof. Only to brighten a moment later, laugh out loud, or surprise someone with a firm embrace.

Emotional turbulence was, of course (the Masters reasoned), an unavoidable side effect to the girl's demanding course of study. What else could they expect from a young woman capable of grasping – simultaneously – both Cantor's continuum hypothesis and mathematical Platonism? Or of recalling – in excruciating detail – what it felt like to die in battle both as, for example, a proud defender of the Orange Free State and as a Basotho child? It was for this reason, after all, that the human mind had evolved to remember only selectively. For this reason that experience became symbolic, then relative, that memories receded, that they sometimes altogether disappeared. Forgetting was as simple a defence mechanism as sex, or flight, the evolution of which (as the girl concurred) could be traced back to the very origin of the species . . .

It is not, perhaps, so surprising, then, that as the years continued to pass, and the question (how best to preserve 200,000 years of accumulated knowledge?) remained unanswered, it also became less pressing. Enthusiasm for the programme had long since waned, funding was siphoned to more immediate projects and concerns, and the girl continued to suffer from brief, interruptive flashes of darkness. A general despondency and a sense of collective defeat settled over the twenty-two remaining Masters – though some optimistically maintained that the 'flashes' marked not a limit, but an as-yet-unexplored direction for the programme. They implored the girl to describe – as minutely as possible – these periods of 'absolute darkness', hoping she might offer some clue as to what was on 'the other side'.

She always left them disappointed.

The problem – she explained – was that she could never quite recall the darkness as it actually occurred, but only in relation to *what happened next* . . .

The less optimistic Masters coughed – or shifted uncomfortably in their seats. For some time now, it had been gallingly difficult for the girl to recall anything abstract – especially anything of a precognitive nature – without falling back on the bad habit of metaphor. She had also become increasingly prone to either conflating events or recalling only their *general themes* – and it was irritating even to the optimists among them that she insisted on relating everything from the limited first person, as if the whole of human history had actually happened to *her*.

Inevitably, whenever these shortcomings were discussed, one of the Masters would – in a wry voice that was deliberately impossible to read – remind them all that 'Whirlwind III had never, after all, been anything but a temporary solution'.

'Yes,' another would reply dolefully. 'And since we're no closer to a better one, perhaps it's time to start with a clean slate?'

'And do away with 200,000 years of accumulated human knowledge?' another would gasp. 'Even *accepting* that "the record" has undergone, in the last few years . . . ahem . . . a slight process of revision, it hardly seems like a decision one could *reasonably* make.'

'We've simply invested too much time and money into this programme to pull out now,' another would confirm. And that would be the end of it – at least for a while.

One day, a philologist spoke up. She was among the more timid of the group and had rarely, until this point, contributed to the debate.

'It may be,' she said – into a rare lull – 'that we are overlooking a basic fact.'

Everyone turned, surprised, and looked at the philologist.

'And what is that?' demanded an attorney of law.

Ignoring the question – and purposely avoiding looking the attorney in the eye – the philologist continued.

'Just because,' she said, 'the subject of our study has so far been compelled to fall back on metaphor does not *mean,* at least necessarily, that the memories themselves actually exist that way. Language, after all, is not designed to either imitate or replace, but instead to *represent* the objects of our experience. It's a complicated code – purposely indirect. Intended to suggest *affinity* rather than to reproduce substantial structure.'

'Are you suggesting,' a philosopher asked cautiously, 'that the subject is merely a veiled reference to the object?'

'That she exists only as a sort of cypher?' a cryptanalyst put in excitedly, 'which, if properly decoded, could point us towards the unbiased historical record, which, as you seem to be suggesting, and despite our inevitable biases – beneath it all – *actually exists*?'

'That it is just a matter of getting – beyond language – to what the language was designed to simultaneously obscure and convey?'

In a voice that suggested that the conversation had strayed, a psychoanalyst turned to the 'subject' herself, who (though forgotten) had been present all along, and asked her to recount her earliest memory.

A statistician groaned. 'And what will that prove?'

'Shhhhhhh!' a poet replied.

A deafening silence ensued and, after several minutes had ticked slowly by, even the optimists began to assume that the girl was suffering from another petit mal. Either that, or she simply had nothing to say.

But then – so quietly that some of the Masters failed to hear – the girl said a single word: 'Imagine.' And then nothing more for such a long time that even those that had heard began to suspect that they hadn't.

'Imagine,' the girl said again. 'Imagine you are looking at a painting of a landscape and suddenly you are not yourself at all, looking at the painting of the landscape, but you are the landscape itself. Or the small glint of light, for example, on the waves in the far corner of the landscape's frame . . .'

As she spoke, her voice began to gain confidence, then speed. 'Imagine being just that,' she said. 'Just the brushstroke – without thought to the brush, or the hand . . .'

When she had finished speaking – and though they had come no closer to a solution, and nothing at all had been 'proven' – the Masters were forced to admit, once again, that despite the girl's 'episodes', an incurable dependence on metaphor and a tendency to lapse (as above) into near-uninterpretable lyricism, her capacity for retaining – and sometimes expressing – the breadth and complexity of human experience remained nothing short of extraordinary.

'And that alone,' remarked a physicist, by way of closing, 'is a reason to continue the programme. One does not, after all, pursue science, or any other worthwhile human endeavour, with anything like a "guarantee". One pursues it only with the sense – a sense that all of us have had, at one point or another, here – that one has touched upon the extraordinary.'

Despite – or because of – the Masters' continued, if faltering, faith, the girl was increasingly plagued by flashes of darkness and fits of dread. She imagined being subjected, at an undesignated point in the future and by an unknown adversary, to some terrible inquisition – and wondered how much, after so many years of silence, she would be willing to withhold.

She was visited by nightmares, hardly slept; her health suffered terribly. Once again the physicians were called, and once again they reported that the girl was in perfect health; that 'nothing' was wrong. In the end, she diagnosed her condition herself: 'the return of the repressed'.

If she only had some outlet, she sobbed – some way of relating her experiences . . . creatively, perhaps! *Yes!* Perhaps that was the answer! She could translate her experiences – everything she had felt and learned – into something else altogether. She could invent a whole other language if necessary! So that (though perhaps recognizable in certain parts) whatever it was she ultimately managed to express would be utterly transformed, virtually impossible to trace . . .

The Masters shook their heads.

But could they even imagine? the girl cried. Had they no empathy at all?

'Think of it!' she begged. '200,000 years of accumulated knowledge, and no one to talk to – no one who even tries to understand! It's enough to drive one positively mad.'

But regulations had only tightened since the project began and the creative arts (as the Masters soon informed the girl) had always been particularly inconvenient for exactly the reason to which she herself referred. It was impossible to regulate. There was simply no way of anticipating if – or in what way – its meaning might one day be interpreted, conveyed or misused.

It was not long after this that the girl did go mad. At least, this was the only explanation offered by even the most optimistic Masters for why – instead of darkness, or faded picture-postcard memories of the past – the future began to flare up suddenly before her, in brief hallucinatory flashes.

At first, she had trouble differentiating these bewildering new 'episodes' from the others, but she soon began to notice that where even her most abstract memories always appeared in the guise of some external image, or object, and she could only ever experience 'absolute darkness' in terms of what it was not, the future was generated from somewhere inside her, existed only in positive terms, and was hers alone.

And yet, despite the thrill of freedom she felt at encountering – for the first time in living memory – what lay beyond living memory, the first thing the girl foresaw was her own annihilation.

'There will come a time,' she announced to the Masters one afternoon, 'that, for the precise reason that you once honoured and celebrated my tremendous gift, you will turn against me.

'Even now,' she warned, 'I have already become too dangerous for you, and my memories – rather than a resource or a point of pride – have become a risk, a liability. Even I cannot tell you what, if captured, I would or would not say. I am, after all, only flesh and blood – no more resistant to abuse or simple boredom than any one of you . . .

'Who knows what little it might take to make me talk? As you know, I have complained often of my own great loneliness – my urge to unburden myself of all that I know . . .

'This will occur to you,' said the girl, sadly. 'It is occurring to you now. Very soon, the risk will strike you as simply too great for the sake of the simple past. There is, after all (you will think) the future to consider . . .

'And this is it. Before our adversaries have the opportunity to do so, it is you who will destroy me. You will end what you began, having come no nearer to your goal. And I cannot blame you.

'Because – when I think back to everything that has happened, to all the decisions I made, or failed to make; to the wars I helped to win or lose; to the thousands of children I bore, to the mistakes I made, the lovers I lost, or, against my better judgement, kept; to the ideas I had and discarded; to the faith that was born, then lost, then born again – on so many different occasions, and in so many ways . . .

'When I remember what it felt like to be a simple splash of light on a painting of a landscape I have never seen – to be just that simple contrast between darkness and light – to be the product of every imagination, and every hand . . .

'When I remember what it felt like to be just an empty waiting thing, when there was nothing to wait for, nothing yet to begin . . . I cannot blame you. Because at every moment there is only one decision, and that is the decision made by every moment – in deepest ignorance – as it returns to what it has not yet been.

'You will make this decision, just as you have made every other: in perfect darkness. Because that is the future – which I have seen and foretold.'

The Masters bowed their heads. They felt embarrassed for themselves, and for the girl, and then ashamed. Because somehow they all felt certain that what she said was true.

Finally, the oldest among them cleared her throat. 'If you are right,' the old Master said, 'and the future is – by contrast to the present or the past – of our own making, why choose to speak of your own demise? I cannot help but be reminded of the old tale – I forget where I heard it now . . . the tale of the bridge, across which you were permitted to pass only if you told the guard in advance where you were going and why, and swore on oath that whatever you said was true. If you swore the truth, you were permitted to pass, but if you swore falsely, you would die on the gallows. There was no chance of pardon.

'One day, a young man came along who swore an oath before crossing that he would die on the gallows. His oath perplexed the judge and jury, because they knew that if the man was allowed to pass freely then he would have lied – and so, according to law, must die; but that if they hanged him, he would have been telling the truth – and so, according to the law, must be set free . . .'

'I am afraid,' said another of the Masters, rising and glancing nervously about – including in the direction of the girl, though she did not appear to be listening – 'that this long story is not at all to the point . . .'

'On the contrary,' the old Master said, 'is it not possible that we are faced, once again, with the decision of whether or not to bind ourselves to truth by death or to pass by lies? As well as with the questions, which path is more honest in the end? And by whom, or by what, are we judged?' ■

Armand Garnet Ruffo

Wallace Stevens's Memory

In a pub down the road from the village of Criccieth
in Wales, the farmers looked me over suspiciously
until I opened my mouth and ordered a beer
and they understood that I was not English.
They continued their conversation in Gaelic
and more or less ignored me. I carried a book
by Wallace Stevens and turned to the last poem
called 'A Mythology Reflects Its Region'
in which he laments in a last gasp that 'Here
In Connecticut, we never lived in a time
When mythology was possible'. It was
a line that signaled absolute forgetting
and it made me want to weep into my drink
for the Mohegan, Mahican, Minisink, Nipmuc,
Pequot, Quiripi, as his gold-feathered bird
in the broad-leafed palm at the end
of a manicured lawn sang of a life
emptied of life.

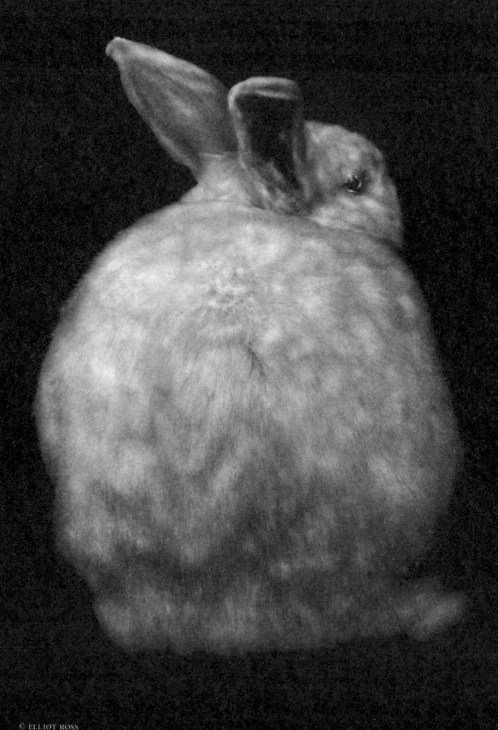

LAGOMORPH

Alexander MacLeod

Some nights, when the rabbit and I are both down on the floor playing tug of war with his toy carrot, he will suddenly freeze in one position and stop everything, as if a great breakthrough has finally arrived. He'll look over at me and there will be a shift, his quick glance steadying into a hard stare. I can't escape when he does this and I have to look back. He has these albino eyes that go from a washed-out bloody pink ring on the outside through a middle layer of slushy grey before they dump you down into this dark, dark red centre. I don't know, but sometimes when he closes in on me like that and I'm gazing down into those circles inside of circles inside of circles, I lose my way, and I feel like I am falling through an alien solar system of lost orbits rotating around a collapsing, burning sun.

Our rabbit – my rabbit now, I guess – he and I are wrapped up in something I don't completely understand. Even when I imagine that I am reading him correctly, I know that he is reading me at the same time – and doing a better job of it – picking up on all my subconscious cues and even the faintest signals I do not realize I am sending out. It's complicated, this back and forth. Maybe we have been spending a little too much time together lately. Maybe I have been spending a little too much time thinking about rabbits.

As a species, let me tell you, they are fickle, stubborn creatures, obsessive and moody, quick to anger, utterly unpredictable and mysterious. Unnervingly silent, too. But they make interesting company. You just have to be patient and pay close attention and try hard to find the significance in what very well could be their most insignificant movements. Sometimes it's obvious. If a rabbit loves you or if they think you are the scum of the Earth, you will catch that right away, but there is a lot between those extremes – everything else is in between – and you can never be sure where you stand relative to a rabbit. You could be down there looking at an animal in grave distress, a fellow being in pain, or, almost as easily, you might be sharing your life with just another bored thing in the universe, a completely comfortable bunny who would simply prefer if you left the room.

Most of the time, none of this matters. We carry on our separate days and our only regular conversations are little grooming sessions during which I give him a good scratch between the ears, deep into that spot he cannot reach by himself and, in return, he licks my fingers or the back of my hand or the salt from my face.

But today is different. Today we have crossed over into new, more perilous territory and, for maybe just the next five minutes, we need a better, more reliable connection. For that to happen, he will have to do something he has never done before, move against his own nature and produce at least one clear sound with one clear purpose behind it. I need this rabbit to find words, or whatever might stand in for words. I need him to speak, right now, and tell me exactly what the hell is happening.

I t is important to establish, before this begins, that I never thought of myself as an animal person. And since I do not come from a pet family, I never thought the family we were raising needed any more life running through it. Especially not a scurrying kind of life, with its claws tap-tap-tapping on the hardwood floors.

The thing you need to understand – I guess it was the deciding factor in the end – is that my wife, Sarah, is dramatically allergic to cats. Or at least she used to be. By this I mean only that she used to be my wife and then, later on, my partner. Like everybody else, we changed with the times and when the new word came in – probably a decade after we'd been married in a real church wedding – we were glad to have it. We felt like a 'partnership' described our situation better, more accurately, and, to be honest, we'd never really known how anybody was supposed to go around being a wife or a husband all the time.

But I'm not sure what terminology you could use to describe what we are now. 'Amicably separated' maybe, or 'taking a break', but not divorced, not there yet. The legal system has not been called in. Sarah and I are not ex-partners. We still talk on the phone almost every day and we try to keep up with the news of everybody else, but it has already been more than a year, and I have never been to her new place in Toronto, the condo on the thirty-fourth floor.

I can imagine her there though, going through the regular Saturday morning. It is probably pretty much the same as it used to be. I see her walking from one room to the next and she has a magazine or her phone in one hand and a cup of tea in the other. She looks out a high window, maybe she contemplates traffic. I don't know. Really, she could be doing anything with anybody. Every possibility is available to her, just as it is for me, and only a few things are non-negotiable any more. Like the allergy. Unless there has been a medical procedure I don't know about, then wherever she is and whatever she's doing, Sarah remains, almost certainly, allergic to cats.

Her condition is medically significant, EpiPen serious, so the cat option was never there for us. And even the thought of a dog, a dog with its everyday outside demands – the walks and the ball-throwing and the fur and the drool and the poop bags in the park – that was always going to be too much, too public, for me.

If we had stayed like we were at the start, if it had been just the two of us all the way through, I think we might have been able to carry on forever and nothing would have happened. The problem was our children, three of them, all clustered in there between the ages of seven and thirteen. They were still kids at this time. It was the moment just before they made the turn into what they are now.

When I look back, I see this was the peak of our intensity together, a wilder period than even the sleepless newborn nights or the toilet training. I don't know how we survived for years on nothing but rude endurance. It was probably something automatic, the natural outcome of great forces working through us. We were like a complicated rainforest ecosystem, full of winding tendrils, lush, surging life and steaming wet rot. The balance was intricate and precise and we were completely mixed up in each other's lives, more fully integrated than we would ever be again.

The kids had been pushing and pushing us and eventually we just gave in. All the friends had animals, all the neighbours and the cousins. There were designer wiener dogs and husky pups with two different-coloured eyes and hairless purebred cats. It felt like there was no way to escape the coming of this creature.

We started with the standard bargain aquarium set-up and a cheap tank bubbled in our living room for about a month and we drowned a dozen fish in there. After that, there was brief talk about other possibilities, but in the end, the rabbit felt like our best option, a gateway to the mammal kingdom. Better than a bird or a lizard, we agreed, more personality, more interaction.

'Maybe a rabbit is kind of like a cat.' I remember saying those words.

We got him from a Kijiji ad – 'Rabbit available to a good home' – and the Acadian man who once owned him ended up giving him to us for free.

I went to his house and visited his carpeted basement. I learned all about the food and the poop and the shedding.

'Is there anything special we need to do?' I asked. 'We don't have any experience.'

'You just don't eat the guy,' the man said. 'Rabbits are right there, you know, right on that line.'

He made a kind of karate-chopping motion, his hand slicing down through the air.

'You either want to be friends with them or you want to kill them and eat them for your supper. We had two other people come here already today. And I was going to take the ad down if you were the same as those bastards. I could see it in their eyes, both them guys. I could just tell. They'd have taken him home and probably thrown him in a stew, a *fricot*, like my *grand-mère* used to make, you know? Hard to look at, I tell you, when somebody's lying to your face like that.'

I asked him what he saw when he looked in my eyes.

He laughed and bonked his temple with his finger.

'I got no clue,' he said.

'All we can ever do is guess, right? No way to ever be sure about what's going on up there. But me, thinking about you right now? Me, I'm guessing that you are not the guy who is going to kill our Gunther.'

'Gunther?' I said.

He crouched down and said the word three times very quickly and he made a clicking noise with his tongue.

The rabbit came flying out from beneath the sofa and went over to the man and stretched up to get his scratch between the ears.

'He knows his name?'

'Of course he does. Doesn't everybody know their own name?'

'And do we have to keep that one?'

'You do whatever you want, my friend. After you leave here, he's going to be your rabbit. But if you want him to know when you're talking to him, I think you better call him what he's always been called.'

I stretched out my hand and Gunther sniffed at my fingers, then gave me a quick lick. His tongue seemed so strange to me then. So long and dry. The tongue of a rabbit is very long and very dry.

The man smiled.

'That there is a very good sign,' he said. 'Doesn't usually happen like that. Gunther, he is usually shy around new people. Normally takes him a little while to make up his mind.'

The rabbit pushed his skull against my shin, scratching an itchy part of his head on the hard bone running down the front of my leg.

I felt the change coming.

'So we have a deal, then?' the man said.

'I think so,' I said. And we shook hands.

'And you're promising me you will not kill him?' He kind of laughed that part at me.

'Yep,' I said, and I shook my head. It was all ridiculous.

'Maybe you can say the real words to me, right now, out loud?'

There was no joke the second time. He looked at me hard and I stared back. He had not yet let go of my hand and as we were standing there I felt the little extra compression he put around my knuckles, the way he pushed my bones together.

'I promise I will not kill Gunther.'

'That is very good,' the man said and he smiled and then he shrugged. 'Or at least, I guess that is good enough for me.'

It took maybe three weeks before Sarah and I started talking about putting him down.

'This isn't working,' she said. 'Right? We can both see that. Whatever happens – we try to sell him or we take him back or to a shelter or whatever, I don't care – but it cannot go on like this. It's okay to admit we made a mistake.'

The kids had already lost interest and the litter box was disgusting. We were using a cheaper kind of bedding and Gunther hated it. In the first couple of days he'd already shredded up two library books and chewed through half a dozen cords without ever electrocuting himself. There was an infection too, something he'd picked up in the move. Maybe we gave it to him, but it was horrible to look at. He had this thick yellow mucus matting down the fur beneath his eyes and both his tear ducts were swollen green and red. He hardly ate anything and instead of the dry, easy-to-clean pellets of poop we'd been promised, he was incontinent. For about a week, our white couch, the couch we still have, the couch where Gunther and I still sit while we watch TV, was smeared with rabbit diarrhoea.

It was getting bad for me too. Something in my breathing had started to change and a case of borderline asthma was settling deep into the membranes of my chest. I felt this strange tenderness blooming in my lungs – like a big bruise in the middle of me – and I was starting to have trouble walking up or even down the stairs in the mornings. We weren't sure of the cause, yet, and it couldn't be pinned directly on Gunther. The doctors said there were other possible explanations – adult-onset conditions – that could stay dormant in your body for decades before springing up fresh in your later life. I had my own wheezing theories, though, and I felt pretty certain that this rabbit and I were not meant to be together.

We took him to a veterinarian who couldn't help us at all.

The guy plunked Gunther down on the stainless-steel examination table and he shone that light into his eyes and his ears and felt around, up and down Gunther's whole body. It took less than ten minutes. Then he snapped off his purple gloves and threw them into a sterile waste basket.

'Look,' he said, 'I've got to be honest here.'

He cocked his head towards the door. On the other side, in the waiting room, there were at least ten other people, all sitting there with their leashes and their treats and their loved ones.

'I think you can see, we're pretty much running a cat and dog shop here. You know what I mean? That's 95 per cent of what we do. And I'm afraid we don't have a lot of experience with the exotics.'

'Exotics?' I said. 'What, is a rabbit exotic now?'

'It is for me. I'm just telling you: I've given you the standard examination that comes with our basic billing package. The next step is going to be X-rays and advanced diagnostics and I don't think you really want to go there. Not for a rabbit anyway. Not for a rabbit that hasn't even been fixed.'

In that moment, it was almost over. Gunther was nearly part of our past. The way to a different version of the future, a new opening, was right there.

'Listen,' he said. 'How about I give you the room for a little while and maybe you can have some time to think about how you'd like to say goodbye. When I come back, if you're good with it, I can give him a little sedative that will calm everything down. Then we set up the IV and whenever you want to release the drug, that will be it; it'll all be over in a painless, quiet, peaceful way. If he can't eat and he isn't drinking and he can't see, what kind of a life is that?'

As he left the room, I watched him shifting his facial features, moving from the serious life-and-death mode he'd been using on us to the cheerful semi-annual check-up face he used for his regular clients.

I turned back to Sarah, but she was already packing Gunther up to bring him home.

'Fuck that guy,' she said to me.

I smiled and nodded my head. My wife does not like to be bossed around by anyone.

We took Gunther home and she got to work on the computer. Online she found a woman in the country who was kind to us, but no nonsense. She was a real farm vet – herds of cattle, giant pigs, even racehorses – and she rarely worked with pets, but she sold us the antibiotics we needed for twenty-five dollars flat and she told us exactly what to do. There were teeth problems, she said. Severely overgrown teeth, looping inside Gunther's head, cutting him every time he tried to chew. The infection had started in his mouth. The other guy had never even looked in there.

'It's not pretty right now,' the vet said. 'And I'm not going to touch anything, but once it's cleared a little, after the medicine has worked, you're going to have to cut them back.'

All of this really happened to us, to Sarah and to me. For an entire week, we fed Gunther with a plastic syringe. In our food processor, we blended up this disgusting kale smoothie with the medication mixed into it. Then I wrapped the rabbit's squirming body in a towel and held him against my chest, squeezing all four of his legs into me. His hair came out, sometimes in thick clumps, sometimes in a kind of fine translucent fuzz that floated through the room and, for sure, penetrated deep into my own body. Sarah forced open his mouth and she drove tube after tube of that green sludge into him. He tried to spit it back up, but most of it went down and the rest dribbled over his chin where it later hardened into this thick green grit in his fur.

But the drugs worked and a week later, when he had his strength back, Sarah and I switched places and did as we'd been told. She held him in the towel and I took a brand-new pair of wire cutters – purchased and sterilized just for this task – and I peeled back Gunther's gums.

You could see it right away. It's easy to tell when things are almost perfectly wrong. Each of his two front teeth was a brownish-yellow tusk, like a miniature ram's horn, curved backwards almost to a full circle with a black streak of what seemed like a blood vessel flowing inside of it. I tried to imagine how things should look if they did not look like this and I tried to summon up a picture for how a rabbit's teeth are supposed to be, although I had never seen a rabbit's tooth before.

Then I just did it. I picked a spot and I aimed the scissor point of the pliers and tried to hit it. Gunther was furious, snorting hard through his nose. Sarah could barely hold him, but even in that moment of crisis he could not generate anything more than a cough.

'Go!' she said. 'Do it right now. Now. Come on.'

I brought the cutters down on the surface of the bone and I squeezed hard and quick, but the tooth was much, much softer than I expected. There was a snap and a section an inch and a half long flew across the girls' room. The second piece, snipped from the second tooth, was a little longer, and it nearly went down his throat before I flipped it free with the tip of my own finger. I dipped my hand in and out of Gunther's mouth. But then it was done and Sarah let him go and he fled beneath the bed.

We were standing there together, Sarah with the soiled towel – Gunther had let go of everything – and me with the pliers in my hand and the chunks of rabbit teeth on the floor. I turned and plucked a piece of fur out of her eyebrow and I remember that she put the towel down and wiped her palms down the front of her shirt, then mine.

'That was not what I expected,' she said.

'Me neither,' I said.

Beneath the bed, Gunther remained perfectly silent. A stranger, entering the room, would not have known he was even there, and neither of us could tell if he was in agony under the mattress or if he felt any kind of relief.

'What do we do now?' I asked.

'I don't know,' she said. 'I guess we wait.'

Somehow it worked the way it was supposed to. With the medicine kicking in and his teeth fixed, Gunther returned to his regular diet of raw Timothy hay. Eventually his poop hardened up and his eyes cleared. Even the kids came back to him. They played games together now, flinging his carrot across the room for fetch, and they worked up a pretty funny matador routine. If you shook a dish towel at him and shouted 'Toro! Toro! Toro!', Gunther would come charging across the room and blast under the fabric. This also worked great with a pyramid of plastic cups. As soon as you built it up, he'd come barrelling through, with real strength and purpose.

When a rabbit is truly happy, they do these insane joyful leaps where they launch their whole bodies way up into the air, so much higher than you think they can go. They twist in odd ways and kick all four of their legs at the same time. It's like one of those ecstatic convulsions you see in born-again churches when people are so moved by the Spirit they can't control their limbs. Gunther used to do that all the time after the bullfight game or the plastic pyramid. That kind of jumping is called a binky. That is the real, technical term for it: binky.

You can never be sure, but I think that somewhere in the blur between our decision at the vet's office and the thing with the teeth and the end of everything else, Gunther's life fit into ours and we all almost made sense. He receded into the deep background of our existence, and took up his place in the daily sequence. Taking care of him became a set of regular tasks. Each week it was a different person's job to change the bedding and blast the room with the Dustbuster and make sure his water and food were topped up. Allowances were paid for this labour and Gunther became a formal responsibility of the household, like emptying the dishwasher or taking out the garbage. When other things, new emergencies, claimed us – the year Sarah's father got sick and eventually died, or the time I was laid off for eight months, or the spring when we had to take out another loan to fix the roof and repoint the chimney and replace all the gutters – I could almost forget that Gunther lived with us. Though we shared the same space, and his presence eventually put me on regular inhalers, puffers that became automatic, I still might go an entire week without actually seeing him. We were all just barely touching and it seemed like the minivan was always running in our driveway, its rolling side door gaping for the quickest possible turn-around, like an army helicopter. Sarah or I would take one step across the threshold of the front door, before we'd be clapping our hands and yelling: 'Let's go! Let's go! Let's go!'

Back and forth through the van door, into and out of traffic. Every day and every night of the week there was some other activity. Making lunches for picky, ungrateful people: whenever I cut the crusts off a sandwich or allowed someone to return a perfectly untouched, but perfectly prepared, Tupperware container of sliced cucumbers and ranch dip, I wondered if I was loving a child or wrecking her for the future. Every morning we just barely made it to the corner for the first school bus at 7.30 and the second at 7.45. Then showering and getting your hair okay and putting on real clothes and going to work and dealing with all the stupid people at work. The stupid things that every stupid person said and did.

Piano and swimming and soccer and music and school assemblies. In an effort to spend quality time with the kids, Sarah signed up to be a Girl Guide leader. She learned all the promises and she got the uniform and we sold cases and cases of cookies. I coached a boys' soccer team for five years, though I knew nothing about soccer in the beginning. Every morning, the morning arrived just five or six hours after we'd gone down. And every morning, when Sarah and I opened our eyes again, we were already late, already behind.

'What is today?' I'd ask and she'd look at me and blink and stare at me like a stranger. Then she'd turn away or look up to the ceiling as if she were reading a screen, like this was the dentist's office and they had a news crawl running up there.

'Wednesday,' she'd say. 'Wednesday is Pizza Day. No lunches. But then violin, and the after-school thing – some meeting we're supposed to go to about cleaning up the playground – somebody has to be seen to be there. Then, if there's time after that, please God, haircuts. Please. Everybody in this whole house needs a goddamn haircut.'

'Yes.'

'I'm serious,' she said. 'You need a haircut. You look like a homeless person.'

I remember once, maybe five years ago – it was at a retirement party for a lady from Sarah's work – and we snuck out during the speeches and fucked in the minivan, right there, doggie-style, on the third-row Stow 'n Go bench. It was ridiculous but also, absolutely, the right thing to do. There were stained popsicle sticks and food wrappers back there, headphones and Lego, even a long-lost running shoe that we were so glad to find. Sarah held it up triumphantly with one hand, even as she was unbuttoning her pants with the other. 'At last!' she said. 'Remind me not to forget about this when we get home.'

The other cars just sat there by the curb under the street lights and no pedestrians ever walked by to peer through our slightly tinted windows. Inside the van, we were rushed and awkward, but we got what we came for and still made it back in time for the cake, all rezipped and smoothed out.

I don't know what happened to us after that. There was no single event. No dramatic explosion, no other character that wandered into our lives. I think we just wore down gradually, inevitably, and eventually, we both decided we'd had enough and it was time to move on. There must have been something else – a pull from the inside or a signal from the outside – that compelled us in some way, but I'm not sure. Maybe we really did just outlive the possibilities of each other's bodies.

But Sarah and I: we had a good, solid run and I think we came through pretty well. Three kids is not nothing and we carried those people – we carried them from their delivery rooms to their day cares to their schools and through all their summer vacations, all the way down to the fancy dinners we hosted on the nights of their high school graduations. Then, one by one, they left our house for good and, all of us, we never lived together again. Two went to universities in different cities and one moved in with her boyfriend across town and started working at a call centre.

After they left, we were by ourselves again. Together, but by ourselves now, and only Gunther stayed. The change was harder than we expected. There was too much space now and we filled it up with everything that had always been missing. Though there was no one else around, we kept getting in each other's way. I felt like the air inside the house was thickening again, but worse now, like a clear sludge was being slowly poured into every gap in our lives. We had to slog through it every day and every exchange was more difficult than it needed to be. Neither of us would ever watch the other person's shows and there were arguments, real arguments, about who should have the power to decide if an overhead light should be turned off or turned on. I did not like how she chewed her food, the way she incessantly talked about other people behind their backs, her selfishness. And she did not like the way I clicked my pens, the way I was always intruding on her plans, the way I started things, but never finished them. No single can of soup could serve us both.

The conditions were right when the transfer opportunity came. This was a real promotion, national-level stuff – much more money and the right kind of work, at last – the type of thing Sarah had wanted for years. She could not afford to let it pass. 'A chance like this,' she said, and we both knew.

After that, we started talking, quietly at first, about 'making a change' or implementing 'the new plan'. We worked it all out, calm and serious and sad, and then it was decided. The job led the way, but we both knew it was more than that and we were clear about what this meant when we explained it to the kids. We needed to move on and there was no pretending any more, no fudging the truth.

'We just want you to be happy,' our oldest daughter said, and the line stuck in my ear because I'd always thought it was the kind of thing parents were supposed to tell their kids.

We kept the show running for four more months – one last school-less September through to one last all-together Christmas – and then we made the calls in the third week of January. Like everybody else, we wanted to get through Christmas before the chatter started. It was civil and transparent and even kind.

I drove her to the airport and we really did kiss and cry in a parking spot that is reserved for kissing and for crying.

'We just have to do what we have to do,' she told me.

I look at Gunther sometimes and I wonder if he is typical – if he is like or unlike all the others of his kind – the rest of the lagomorphs that populate this world. I wonder if he has even ever seen another rabbit or if he thinks maybe I am a rabbit, too. They are an altricial species – another word I have learned – born blind and deaf and defenceless, so he would have no memory of his siblings or his mother, no sight or sound to carry forward from that first phase of his life. If there is a moment in your existence when you cannot survive without another's timely intervention – if you are like a hatchling bird fresh out of the shell – then you are altricial. When Gunther was born, he would have been a hairless three inches of flesh, a pink wriggling tube in the world, barely more than a mouth and a fragile circulatory system visible through his skin. There might have been eight or nine others with him in the litter. Maybe he still holds some faint feeling of them, the touch of other rabbits, all those teeming bodies pressed up against each other, huddling for heat. That's another word I like: the verb, to teem. You hardly ever get to use it.

There is so much out there. I have scrolled the images on the internet and read the articles and followed the diagrams, the maps that show us what really happens if we follow them down the hole, through the warren and into the complex society they build down there, three feet beneath the place where we live. The largest and most complicated colonies can twist through hundreds of metres of tunnels and switchbacks, a path no predator could ever follow. Guided only by instinct, they dig dark mazes out of the ground, building their real working routes so that they run right beside a series of faked dead ends and false starts. Then they put in dozens of different entrances and escapes, some of them real, some of them decoys. The strategy is amazing, the fact that this level of deception, such advanced trickery, is built right into the great natural plan.

Despite all of this, in the wild, a rabbit gets to live for a year, maybe two. Less than 10 per cent of them ever see that second summer or winter. I guess they are born for dying, a new generation every thirty-one days. But that's not how it is for Gunther. He is fifteen years old now, at least, and I suppose this makes him a nearly unique organism in the history of the world. From here on in, every one of his experiences will be unprecedented.

Today I decided I would try to show him something new. He has always been an indoor pet – a house rabbit – but this morning I brought him outside. There was work I'd been neglecting in the yard and it had to be done. I did not think he would run away – our fences go straight to the ground – but there are gaps that are large enough and I wanted to at least give him a choice.

I put him down on the lawn and gave him a good scratch between his ears.

'There you go,' I said, and I spread my arms wide as if I was granting the yard to him. 'All yours.'

He looked up at me, less enthused than I expected, and then he just lowered his head and pulled up a mouthful of fresh clover and started munching away. He casually turned and hopped a few feet over to sniff at the base of the back porch, near the spot where we keep our compost bin and the garden hose. He did not seem to be in a rush to go anywhere.

I turned away from him and walked towards the shed. I spun the combination on the padlock, opened the door and wheeled out our dusty push lawnmower. I grabbed the snips and the hedge clippers and the sturdy old garden rake with its rectangular grin of sharp tines. I took out the wheelbarrow. For half an hour I purposefully did not look back in the direction where I had left Gunther. I wanted to leave him alone and give him a chance to sort things out for himself.

There had been so many spring Saturdays like this in our past, so many days full of lists, with things that needed to be done and put in order. I raked the dead winter leaves into a pile and I uncovered the beds and I took an initial stab at trimming back the rose bush and the other perennials that Sarah had always kept up. I tried to remember everything she had told me about how to get the angle right on your snips so that everything you cut away grows back and then grows out in the right way. Fullness was what we were always aiming for. We wanted the plants in our backyard to be full, to bloom thick and heavy. I touched each fork where the branches or the stems parted and I paused and thought about what to do. Then I eenie-meenie-miney-moed my way through the decisions, before cutting one side back and letting the other side live.

I turned around just in time. There was a sound, I guess, more of a vibration in the air, but it should not have been enough. I don't know what made me look. It was just a sigh really, a gurgling exhale, like the wheezing my own lungs made at their worst, only more shallow and quicker.

The thing I saw – the thing my eyes landed on – was a completely normal occurrence in the natural world, I guess. But at the same time, it was something shocking – something completely new and troubling – to me. A snake, much thicker and much longer than the kind of animal I believed could live beneath our porch, was spiralled around Gunther's body. The drama was almost over and everything had already shifted to stillness. Gunther was stretched out to his full length and the sound coming from him, the vibration, was the last of his air being squeezed out of his body. The snake had wound round him four or five times and their heads, Gunther's and the snake's, were touching. It seemed almost like they were looking into each other's eyes. Their tails, too, were almost even, but in between – beneath and inside the symmetry of the snake – there was this wretched contortion in Gunther's body, a twisting that seemed to spin his neck in the opposite direction from his front paws. I felt, for sure, that all his bones had already been broken.

I have looked it up – I went immediately to the search engine when I came back to the house – and I know now that this other creature, the thing that once lived beneath our porch, was a rat snake, a non-venomous constrictor, as local to this part of the world, perhaps even more local, than my New Zealand rabbit. I have learned that rat snakes, or corn snakes, make great pets, that they are wonderful with kids, that they are the gentle hit of the reptile show that comes to visit all the schools. Childen love to feel them spiralling around their limbs, the dry, wet sensation of it. The rat snake in my backyard was not at fault, not doing anything wrong. Only taking up its assigned place and following an instinctive pattern it could not choose or change. Gunther too was where he was supposed to be, I guess. When all of this happened, I was the only thing moving out of order. But I could not stop myself from moving.

'No,' I said, and I took four or five purposeful strides towards them. Then I reached out and I picked up this strange and seething combination of whatever it was and I held it in my hand. I do not think I will ever touch something like this again and I do not know what I felt. It wasn't heavy. The two of them together did not weigh as much as a bag of groceries. They were in my left hand and, with my right, I grabbed the snake just behind its head and tried to twist it away, to pry it off of Gunther, to separate them. It turned on me almost instantly, unspooling from Gunther and swivelling onto my arm. I flung both of them back on the ground. Gunther fell and did not move, but the snake immediately began to head towards the pile of leaves, sideways and forward at the same time.

But we were not done yet. I grabbed the rake and followed behind, and when my chance came, I swung the tool hard. It arched over my shoulder and cut down quickly through the air and I felt the resistance as the point of one, maybe two of the teeth penetrated the snake's body almost in the middle. The rake descended all the way through and dug into the ground on the other side. Both ends of the snake, the top and the bottom, kept going, zigzagging furiously, but the middle was pinned down and stationary. I walked to the head, and I waited and watched the swaying. Then I timed it right and I brought my heel down as precisely as I could. I was only wearing running shoes, but I pressed hard and I felt the bones crushing, and the liquid giving way, like stepping on an orange, maybe. But after fifteen seconds, the swaying stopped, the top half of the snake first and then the bottom. I looked back to where I had been just a few seconds before and I was prepared for what I expected to see – the crumpled white pile, unbreathing – but it was not there. Instead, over to the side, maybe two feet away from where he had fallen, Gunther was up and at least partially reinflated back to his regular rounded shape. He was perfectly stationary now, still in the way that only a rabbit can be still, and he was staring at me, staring hard at this scene.

I looked at him and then down at the snake, the length of it, the stretch of its body. The things it had done and the things I had done. I did not know what any of them meant. I did not know what could or could not be justified. I only knew what had happened and that, eventually, I would have to come back here, to this spot, and clean up the mess.

I went over to Gunther and I picked him up as gently as I could, but he gave me no reaction. He was only a soft object in my hands, almost like a stuffed animal, like a kid's toy that is supposed to stand in for a real rabbit, or for whatever a rabbit is supposed to mean. I brought him back inside, back to our house, where we are now, and I put him on the couch and knelt in front of him. I ran my fingers all along his body, like the uncaring veterinarian from years ago, but like him, I couldn't feel anything out of place, and couldn't tell if there was something else wrong, something broken deeper inside of him.

The phone rings and it is Sarah. She lives in a city where it is an hour earlier than it is here, and, for a second, I get confused about time zones and I imagine that none of this has happened to her yet.

'How you doing today?' she says.

The tone is light and easy and intimate. When conditions are right, we can fall right back into who we were. She just wants to chat about nothing, to fill in the time on an empty Saturday morning. It is quiet on both ends and I feel certain that we are both alone, at least for now.

'Well,' I say. It is hard to find the right words. 'Something bad happened with Gunther just now.'

'No,' she says, and the turn comes right away, a panicked edge sharpening her voice. 'What happened?' she asks. 'Is it bad? I was just thinking about him and wondering about the two of you. Is he going to be okay? Are you okay?'

'It was a snake,' I say, trying to make all of this as basic as I can. 'Can you believe that? Like a real snake, a pretty big one, in our yard, and it almost had him, but then he got away. I'm just not sure what's going on with him right now. Maybe he's in shock.'

I make the clicking noise with my tongue and I say the name, the word that once seemed so strange to me. I say 'Gunther' and I wait for him to come but nothing happens.

The phone is pushed against my ear and Sarah's breathing is there.

'Tell me exactly what happened,' she instructs. 'And tell me what he looks like right now. Try to explain it to me. I need details. Maybe we need to call someone.'

'He seems alert,' I say, 'but he's not moving.'

I reach out and stroke the bridge of his nose with my index finger and I feel him nudging back a little bit, trying to meet my skin with his body.

I watch this happening – almost like an extreme close-up running in slow motion, a picture that I am in and observing at the same time – my finger on his nose and his nose against my finger. There is a pause during which nothing happens. Nothing happens and nothing happens, but it goes on for too long and the gap gets too wide. I lose track.

Sarah breaks the silence.

'David!' she shouts. 'David, are you there?'

My name surprises me, like an odd noise coming from another room, something crashing, and at first I don't know how to respond, but before I can do anything, Gunther twists his head, hard and quick, pivoting both ears towards me and the telephone. He recognizes Sarah's voice – the sounds that only she can make – a cry coming out of this plastic receiver, cutting through. He turns and his expression, the shape of his face, the tilt of his head, rearranges into something I have never seen before, flaccid and seized in all the wrong places. But his breathing is strong and steady. I feel like he needs me, like I am the only one who can pull him through.

'I'm here,' I say into the phone, 'but I can't talk right now. I have to let you go.'

I hang up and stare at Gunther and I see myself reflected again at the red centre of his eye. The surface seems cloudier than normal, and I don't think he can process what is happening any more, this hazy mixture of light and frequency that surrounds us – the familiar and the strange. I know he still knows me – he still knows us – and I try to look past my reflection. I imagine moving directly through the membranes and lenses of his eyes, down the nerves and all the way up into his brain. I think our shared past, our lives, are still there, held in his memory. Inside the mind of the oldest rabbit that has ever lived, we are a single thought – vivid and urgent and distinct – but then it passes and the rest is everything else. ∎

© TU HAO CHIN
ashamed of you, 2012

THE INITIALS

Alex Leslie

O n the day of the inquiry, my grandmother stayed home in her apartment, drank red wine on her couch, and watched back-to-back episodes of *The Passionate Eye* on CBC and growled, 'All those goddamn people are crooked anyhow,' and then she ordered in Chinese food and fell asleep for centuries. At the inquiry the man running the show walked to the front of the room and said that he had lost our book of names. My grandmother kept the list of names in the guest room, bottom-left corner of the bookcase. She opened the book and said, 'This is my last birthday,' and fell asleep again, while her apartment building rotated on the bird spine of a sundial. I went to the inquiry but never told her. She wouldn't have liked it. The man at the front said without memories there is no past and furthermore everything you need to know is on *The Passionate Eye* on CBC. I went back home, hands empty. There was no inquiry in the place where her mother was from because they burned the Jewish men on the beaches and the Jewish women were the smoke. 'Do you know how to name children?' my grandmother said to me. 'You take the initials of their dead relative and use them again and again so that the letters are never lost.' This is written in a secret language. I often slept in her guest room except when I slept on the couch in the living room. I realized that the upholstery was patterned with her initials when

I woke up to find her initials tattooed into my cheek. Alphabet welts, they faded but stayed. 'Don't sleep on the couch,' she said. 'It'll make you achy all over and besides we don't get tattoos in this family.' She showed me the magic trick to remove the core from an apple without moving any of her fingers. She opened her mouth and gold coins fell out. There was no inquiry and no report either because we all have new names now. We took our names from the book in the guest room or we wrote our names down in a guestbook, we can't remember which, and there is no record of the threshold. When I got home from the inquiry I lay down on my own bed and fell asleep. When I woke up *The Passionate Eye* was on CBC again, part of a series she would have loved about Hillary Clinton and empowered female leaders. The next day we released her remains and the day after that it had been a whole year since her death. I received a book in the mail. All the rest had been sold or given away or disappeared. This book, hidden in my grandmother's needlepoint, made it across the ocean in the belly of a ship. A person with a jug. A boy squatting in shorts. There is no record of the boat's arrival. She always said she didn't know very much about what had happened, nothing that would be of much use anyway. An amnesiac with a stomach full of facts. I read the book but couldn't find my name, so I looked for my initials instead and suddenly they were everywhere, a survival of stars. I could remember every moment of the inquiry but nothing that had happened and no words that had been spoken. I'd sat in the front row and taken notes like I always do because it is important to have a record, but only the first letter of every word, all of the initials. There was no inquiry for my grandmother's relatives and the place they came from because she only used Yiddish to speak with her sister and with the dead. It isn't a secret but it isn't much of a history either. Only speak to yourself in a language only you can understand, and then you can put it away forever. The inquiry went on for a long time, until it was finished. No records were released until the nineties and photos taken by the Extraordinary Commission are as blurry as images of interstellar travel or smoke as it leaves a mouth, so who can really tell. It went on for a while and I was the last one to speak and I forgot everything I wanted to know, and said, 'I'm sorry, I have to go, I'm late for the ferry to the island to go see my grandmother.' The line-up for the ferry was longer than it had ever been before. I waited for weeks and weeks, inching forward, past turnstile after turnstile, all the rows of cars winding around one another, so that I couldn't see where the line began or ended. Service had been horrible ever since the ferries went corporate. Finally I got to the front of the line and a BC Ferries employee leaned across her desk and snapped at me, 'Where ya goin? Duke Point or Departure Bay?' I said, 'I'm looking for the boat with the book.' She said, 'It's Duke Point you want then,' and gave me my ticket. It was very still. The parking lot stretched flat in all directions and I watched the people walk back and forth with their cups of Starbucks coffee and hot dogs in luminous foil wrappings. I watched a woman at the chain-link fence tell her dog to piss, command him like a soldier, kick at the mud in frustration. I watched a father tighten the yellow ropes over the top of his car to keep all his family's stuff strapped on tight so their camping gear wouldn't slide into the waves. I watched some children scream mindlessly, standing in a circle, small faces bright with cold. A bird fell out of the sky. I watched the ocean glow with its own secret light. Everybody rushed for their cars when the huge white metal boat appeared, the ramps attached to it like mechanical arms. Smoke drifted up off the water and got into all of our nostrils and eyes. Over the speakerphone system, the woman who'd sold me my ticket said, 'There was no inquiry because she died before you learned how to write this poem,' and I waited for the boat to start loading, scanned my iPhone newsfeed for updates, stared at all the unanswered messages from friends. When the boat was ready, the line of cars started to move forward. We were all going somewhere new. In the back of the car was everything I'd ever written in paper bags, the first letter of every word circled so that I would remember how to read it even while sleeping. As long as the initials are stable, other things can move around as much as they want. My grandmother came walking off the ramp from the boat, holding a bottle of wine. She walked down the line of cars and everybody held their cups out the windows of their cars and she filled the cups one by one as she walked. She filled every cup less than halfway, so no one would drink too much while they were driving. She did not indulge and never touched the glass or the car with her fingers. She came to my window and I held out my cup and she filled it all the way to the brim without meeting my eyes and then the wine came pouring over the edges of the cup, red over my fingers, and she kept going down the line of cars. In the rear-view mirror, her body was very, very small. There was no inquiry because nobody knew where they were going or what was going to happen or how long it would take. It's a simple story. She vanished into the flat grey line of the parking lot's horizon, where the cement met the ocean in a blur, something solid becoming light. After she was gone, all the cars started to move again. I drove onto the ferry drinking from my cup. Like I always do, I went out onto the ferry deck and the salt wind sandblasted me clean. ■

mslexia
WRITER'S DIARY

- monthly 'blue-sky' writing exercises to stretch your imagination
- weekly reading recommendations and inspirational quotes from world-renowned authors
- need-to-know directory of resources for writers
- professional guide to manuscript layout and editing symbols
- list of key competitions, festivals and awards in the literary year
- pitch calendar to help you develop seasonal submissions
- submissions tracking section
- lots of blank pages for ideas
- PLUS all the basic diary features, including week-to-view pages and A-Z contacts section

Our *Mslexia* Writer's diary is back and this year's theme is blue-sky thinking. We're looking at creativity: where it comes from, what it is, how to access and optimise it – and follow it through to a complete piece of work.

Following our sell-out 2017 diary, order yours today!

Writer's Diary 2018
£13.99 (plus p&p)

mslexia.co.uk/diary
0191 204 8860

Fanny Britt with her sons, Hyppolyte (left) and Darius (right), in Madison Square Park, New York, 2017
Courtesy of the author

WRITING WHILE WORRIED

Fanny Britt

TRANSLATED FROM THE FRENCH BY PABLO STRAUSS

H*e's grown so tall, so thin*, I thought, wetting a cloth under the bathroom tap. My older son was kneeling on the cement tiles, holding back his long reddish-brown hair. He'd been dry-heaving for over an hour. He was hot, he was cold, and now and then I could just barely hear a little moan. He's not one for drama.

I wrung out the cloth and laid it on his neck – *look how his shoulder blades stick out!* – and sat up with him on the rim of the tub. It was 2.47 a.m. and we'd been up since 12.30, since I'd heard tiptoes on the bunk-bed ladder, its every creak familiar and for years bound up with the ebb and flow of my own sleep. *Someone's awake, someone's wheezing, someone's coughing.* He must have caught a virus from a door handle or a library book. Who knows? He's almost fifteen, I can't follow him everywhere, have to settle for repeating directions – *Wash your hands!* – and hope for the best.

Sitting on the bathtub staring at the crumbling grout between the tiles, *you should have spaced them wider, picked a different colour grout, or is that mould? Can mould make teenagers sick? Will my inability to protect him from danger and indigestion lead to his death? You can't stop death, it comes sooner or later, it must. But I refuse to be witness to my children's deaths, let alone to have played a part in them. What error escaped your attention? What crack went unfilled?* The questions cascaded forth as

I clung for dear life to my whirligig of worry.

> A Wind that rose
> Though not a Leaf
> In any Forest stirred[1]

All this was so terribly normal: I crave worry like a junkie needs a fix. Since childhood I've been powerless to resist, and have taken perverse comfort in being undermined by my familiar foe. Worry bestows intensity with one hand while robbing vitality with the other.

The next day, as my son lay recuperating under a blanket on the living-room sofa – *he didn't die, the sun is out, get on with it* – I sat down and turned on my computer. That day, like every other, I had to chain myself to my desk and do my job. Would I be paralyzed, swallowed up by the hangover of my anxiety, or enjoy the clarity that sometimes descends during moments of crisis? Both were possibilities. I'd seen both before.

Writing does not tolerate interruption. We must return each day to the blank page with all we have inside and salvage something usable, no matter how slight. Getting dumped by a narcissistic lover while plotting a revenge story can be downright instructive; charting my parents' generation's dreams of free love and social equality as their neoliberal parties govern us so cynically, merely frustrating. What makes me persist? Stubbornness, a survival instinct, an unquenchable thirst for putting torment to good use. In thrall to my obsessive fear of losing my children, I wrote a play about what happens when rural services are delocalized – a boy falls, the ambulance comes too late, he ends up in a coma. And my consternation at the bigotry of a small but vocal portion of Quebec's population impelled me to write a graphic novel about vulnerability as a form of courage.

But just as it can spur me on, worry is adept at stifling and silencing. Two years ago marked the twenty-fifth anniversary of the

---

[1] Emily Dickinson, 'A Wind that rose'.

École Polytechnique massacre that took the lives of fourteen women at an engineering school affiliated with the Université de Montréal. I was interviewed for a retrospective with three other women – a journalist named by the killer as another target in his misogynist 'manifesto', a survivor of the mass shooting and young activist who was born after that tragic day. I was twelve when it happened, and though I remember it like yesterday, and still walk daily through the fallout of that horror, like a layer of moss on the ground of my city, I haven't yet found a way to talk about it. As a brutal, boorish regime south of our border takes its place alongside countless others of its ilk around the world, I find myself more and more paralyzed by worry. What can be done to keep from falling silent?

How can we broach horror in fiction when the horror of the real world so far exceeds it? Intoxicated by worry, how is a writer to keep writing?

Maybe in times of darkness the answer is to turn away. Put on a white dress, find a room with a window, watch the seasons change; no longer venture out into the world, but let our voices reach down from atop a staircase; see no more faces, feel no more brushing hands, let no one stand between us and the full unrelenting force of this punishing life – and embrace fear in peace. As a teenager I too felt the lure of asceticism.

> There is a pain – so utter –
> It swallows substance up –
> Then covers the Abyss with Trance.[2]

Swallowed up by her pain, Emily Dickinson spent years alone in her room worrying that her kidneys might fail. They did; she died. Living as a recluse didn't solve a single problem, neither hers nor the world's. But the work she left us, nourished and thwarted by the

---

[2] Emily Dickinson, 'There is a pain – so utter –'.

enemy within, contains multitudes. Did she find love in her poems? Did they love her back? Were they any help at all?

As a young adult I traded in the Abyss and the Trance for a new tragicomic world view, one I've clung to ever since. On the melamine bookshelves of my first apartment you'd find *Invitation to the Married Life*, by Angela Huth, alongside all of Lorrie Moore, spines cracked and yellowed from too much love. Lined up on the wooden bookshelves of my current home are Claire Messud and Lisa Moore and Rachel Cusk and Elizabeth Strout, exacting archaeologists of the subsurface violence of everyday life. I have cherished them each in turn.

The late American writer Laurie Colwin had a knack for depicting how keen love for the things of this world can be folded into pathological pessimism. Countless novelists have chronicled everyday life with humour and pangs of self-knowledge – it is hardly a rare or new approach. But reading Colwin's work was my first encounter with a writer who possessed both lyrical pragmatism and an unflinching clear eye – a combination I've aspired to emulate ever since, in literature and in life. It was she who held up a light to the inner workings of young adulthood and the discontent bred in the bone of a privileged yet decidedly morose society I was forced to recognize as my own. While some of us cherish Colwin's fiction ('My wife is precise, elegant, and well-dressed, but the sloppiness of my mistress knows few bounds'), she is perhaps better remembered for her culinary essays, published in magazines and collected in the plainly titled *Home Cooking: A Writer in the Kitchen* and *More Home Cooking: A Writer Returns to the Kitchen*. They read like precursors of today's food blogs, but what makes them so compelling is not their quintessential New York humour, nor Colwin's ability to capture the zeitgeist of the eighties with entire pages on convoluted searches for organic ingredients that had to be sourced by mail – what would she think of the industrial organics glutting our store shelves today? No, what elevates these occasional pieces is their common sense of purpose. Describing dinner parties gone awry or laying out her recipe for borscht, Colwin is ever the advocate of a life redeemed by the stubborn repetition of the small necessary acts of everyday living.

Cook, eat, clean up, start again. A life of work, tempered by communion.

Colwin staves off worry and existential angst, the very ailments that afflict her fictional characters, by kneading dough, measuring flour and peeling chickpeas. Did this balm somehow make writing and life a little easier to bear? Or is it just me?

O r is it just me. 'Is it you who sees it that way, or is it just there?' asks Margaret Atwood imperiously in a 1984 documentary, *Once in August.* The film-maker, Michael Rubbo, seems convinced that his revered subject must draw on a deep inner well of darkness to write of such toxic personal relationships and a world bereft of hope. Let's set aside the tired premise that a woman who writes can only ever reveal a reflection of her self, while men hold up a mirror to humanity. Left alone with the camera, Atwood sees what's going on: 'He's trying to find out why some of my work is sombre . . . he's trying for some simple explanation of that in me, or in my life.' Look elsewhere, she tells us. Her books are dark because the world's a dark place. As for their author's life – who cares?

Well, me for one. I care.

I don't need to know whether Atwood's writings reflect an inner malaise, but I yearn to understand how one can so presciently see and dissect an entire society as she does, and get on with the business of living. Does the clairvoyance that makes Atwood and Colwin and Dickinson such vital writers beget a perpetual state of weariness and unalloyed tension? And if so, how good a deal is that?

I first saw the Atwood documentary by chance late one night on TV. I was a young author with no text and a baby feeding at my breast – *he is not dead, the sun will rise, get on with it* – riveted to the screen by the scenery. The cottage where Margaret Atwood spent her summers, on an island in the middle of a lake, looked so much like my own childhood cottage that I at first thought it must be the same spot. It had to be Blue Sea Lake, near Maniwaki, in among the birch and black spruce, a hinterland between north and south where pine needles pile up with leaves. As it happens her cottage was about three hours west of ours, deeper and further into the woodland of Témiscamingue. No matter: I loved imagining that she might be cutting the same rhubarb and catching the same crayfish. I was giddy to learn that a writer of such genius could have been raised on the very same landscape as me. Here before me was an ideal writer's life: out for canoe rides, kneeling in the garden, running to the end of the dock and jumping in to cool off before a late-afternoon drink; up early to work in the magical silence of a house where everyone else was still sleeping, then free to while away the rest of the day, lost in life and foliage.

Revisiting the Atwood documentary a few weeks ago, I saw something very different. As a twenty-four-year-old budding writer, I felt I had chanced upon a harmonious arrangement of writing and life. It was like entering a house both lived-in and entirely new – a house of one's own in all its silent glory. Now pushing forty, a mother and author repeatedly confronting my own limits, what struck me was Atwood's agility, her manifest talent for seeing deep into the encroaching darkness – then slipping off to pick watercress in the garden. We see her in the evening, reading *Treasure Island* to her daughter, a tanned girl with a tangled mop of curly hair. We hear her partner's deep voice, haunted as a shipwreck, singing an old sea shanty to lull their daughter to sleep. These are scenes of extraordinary commonness and tenderness. Yet in her writing it's the worst of possible worlds; *The Handmaid's Tale* came out the following year. It must take a rare magic to penetrate so deep into the darkest, densest forest, with no light but words and a makeshift hope, and then emerge so strong. What error escaped your attention? What crack went unfilled? This is my torment, my purpose.

A few weeks after my older son's illness, my younger son woke up with glassy eyes and a hollow cough. It was the end of winter – *he will not die, the sun shines bright, get on with it* – and though a dose of red syrup would lift his spirits, the fever kept him home from school. We went out together, to silence the worry ringing in my ears and to fill his lungs with fresh air. On the little bridge over the locks in Île-de-la-Visitation he gleefully gathered chunks of frozen snow piled alongside the path and threw them off the tip of the Island of Montreal into the Rivière des Prairies. We could see the water running under the snow. Some of the chunks crashed into little ice sheets gathered in haphazard islands, but once in a while one would hit its target, a small hole in the ice, and plunge into the flowing water beneath. Then we'd run across the bridge and watch it shoot the rapids. The water had worn each block down to almost nothing. I had writing to do, later. Later I'd write. ■

Still from *Wolfe and Montcalm*, directed by Allan Wargon, 1957
© National Film Board of Canada

THE BATTLEFIELD

Dominique Fortier

TRANSLATED FROM THE FRENCH BY RHONDA MULLINS

A June night, age nineteen.

It is warm and cool on the Plains. The heat soaked up by the earth that day hovers in the grass just above the ground; the night air carries smells of the river below, grey and silent, scents that speak of whales, eels and starfish.

We run, out of breath, not watching where we step. There is nowhere to go, just the sky overhead. Cap Diamant nearby, with roots of the trees clinging to the cliffs, afraid of tumbling into the abyss. There is something foreign yet familiar about having you by my side. For years, you have been passing through my life; like a comet, disappearing as quickly as you come.

(Was it before or after the Plains? A different year? We were sitting on the ramparts facing the river, watching night fade to dawn. Everything was powder grey: the steeples, the domes and the slim towers of the Petit Séminaire behind us, the Château Frontenac perched on the rock like the woman bending over a well on the bank before us.

We didn't say anything. Try as I might, I can't remember any of our conversations. Our intimacy was beyond words – we were no fools. Ghosts of the Carignan-Salières Regiment marched along the cobbles of the rue des Remparts, bayonets in hand. They were going to throw their bones in the river.

My heart had been broken. And you, who did you love? Boys or girls? Or just books and chess? An extraordinary age of discovery, where everything happens for the first time. This is true of men, women and countries. Others talk about you as one would talk about a figure or a character: sorcerer, angel, ogre. Their perspectives obscure as much as they illuminate. A series of eclipses. You are the sort of person who can be invented.

What I know: you like silence. Your gestures have a quietness that gives your movements the appearance of ritual, simple and solemn. Your pale fingers hovering over the bishop on a chessboard, rolling tobacco into a slim cigarette, stroking a cat whose eyes are half closed. Some people know how to find water, or gold; you know how to find calm. There is always something around you that feels like a drowsiness – a slow waking.)

I don't know what you see in me. It may be that I distract you. Or you don't understand me and that pleases you; you like what eludes you. I've been told that I run fast, but this evening I fly.

We run together, and suddenly I am overcome by a dizzy spell. The night swallows me; I'm going to fall and rather than trying to steady myself, I stick out my foot so that you fall with me. Together we tumble into the grass, a spill that lasts a thousand years.

We lie side by side in the middle of the dark battlefield. You have a throaty laugh, and I have long wondered whether it was mocking or joyful. This evening, it is a gentle cascade rising up to the sky.

Did you kiss me? I don't remember. My lips taste like tobacco and vodka served ice cold in a big, clear glass. Your chest rises and falls as you try to catch your breath. My head in the hollow of your shoulder rises and falls in time. On the other bank, a thousand lights shine from the refinery, a twinkling castle, deserted and golden, turrets breathing fire. The stars in the sky are like grains of sand on the edge of a dark sea. The earth under our backs is warm, having soaked up the blood of Wolfe and Montcalm, their men and their horses.

I don't remember getting up. I am still lying there, by your side, on the bank of the great river, between the dead and the stars. I am still running. I am still falling. ■

LE CIRQUE

Rawi Hage

A circus is fluid in its movements, and has a perpetual love for metamorphosis and disguise. One day, pointing my camera at a trapeze in flying motion, it hit me: a photograph is nothing but a tool to render the world into stillness. To stand and frame the life of a circus, with its history of performing and wandering through markets and palaces, felt like a travesty. I was saddened to find myself committing an act of philosophical and historical injustice. A circus, I thought, should not be represented in its fragments.

Photography advocates motionlessness, I suddenly said to myself. In its celebration of stillness, photography is about halting time. I wondered if it should confine itself to the things that seek to beautify the world or declare the inevitability of our death. Photography, I thought, might be more suitable for recording war, or fashion, since both advocate a triumph over something: the former a triumph over all others, and the latter a triumph over perceived inadequacies of the self. On the other hand, a circus is, historically and in the imagination, a place of refuge for all those rejected, abused or orphaned by war and mayhem. A circus is a travelling nation, disregarding the borders of nation states and the homogeneities of beauty.

How aggressive, I thought, to point my lens at a clown or a freak. How immoral, I thought, was my attempt to invade this place of refuge, but I kept on taking photographs, remembering that I had also left my home to settle in another country, and I was also a refugee who once sought to flee a place that was torn apart by war, I also belonged to the contingencies of rejects. Circuses have the capacity to transform those rejected by society – the acrobats, rope-walkers, puppeteers and expelled demons – into wonders and celebrities.

These images were taken in 2010 just outside of my adopted home, Montreal, at the Carnivàle Lune Bleue, a circus which one day surfaced, performed and moved on. The province of Quebec still hosts many carnivals and circuses. Naturally the function of these events has changed over time and, these days, the rawness of the old, traditional circus exists in tandem with the vivid spectacles of aesthetically wondrous performances, such as those by Cirque du Soleil. However, the question of why the place where I live has hosted, throughout the years, so many circuses – and excelled at them – persists. I suspect that, here, the identity of the rejected is cherished because this land has a history of seclusion and winter, as well as a resistance to all that is overwhelming or that is imposed by the conventional. Laughter, here, was never an escape from the harshness of the land, but a strange kind of defiance. ∎

alto

Éditeur d'étonnant

Eleanor CATTON | Nicolas DICKNER | Dominique FORTIER
Rawi HAGE | Catherine LEROUX | David MITCHELL
Emily ST. JOHN MANDEL | Larry TREMBLAY
Sarah WATERS | Patrick deWITT

© Karoline Georges

Conseil des Arts du Canada
Canada Council for the Arts

editionsalto.com | aparte.info

SODEC
Québec

THE MARTIANS CLAIM CANADA

Margaret Atwood

The Martians descend to Earth in their spaceship. They intend to go to New York – they want to see something called 'a musical' – but they get the directions mixed up, as many before them have done, and end up in Canada instead, as many before them have also done. Specifically, they land on a chunk of rock in the boreal forest somewhere on the Laurentian Shield. There is no one around, or no one you might recognize as 'one'.

'Where is here?' says the first Martian.

' "Where" is always relative,' says the second Martian. 'Where in relation to what?'

'This approach is not helpful,' says the third Martian.

Luckily there is a mushroom – it's the summer, however brief – and these Martians know how to talk to mushrooms, which they resemble somewhat in appearance.

'Where are we?' they ask the mushroom. It is an *Amanita muscaria* – not entirely trustworthy, prone to illusions, and somewhat vain, due to having been worshipped as a deity in Siberia, but it is the only sentient being in evidence.

'Depends who you ask,' says the mushroom. 'And how long their memory is. Mushrooms have long memories. Some of them are thousands of years old. However, they are not always very talkative.'

'We've noticed that,' say the Martians.

'Depends also on what you mean by "here",' says the mushroom. 'Do you include the part underneath ground level? That's mostly what "here" is, for a mushroom.'

'Just the coordinates,' says the first Martian. 'Spell it out for us. And please don't quibble about whether mushrooms know how to spell: it's a figure of speech.'

'If the memory in question is short, this might be a place called Canada,' says the *Amanita*. 'Longer, it might be a place called New France, more or less, maybe, if those people got up this far. Longer than that, it might be a place called Turtle Island. Longer than that, it might be a place called Laurentide Ice Sheet. Longer than that, it might be a place called Laurentia, otherwise known as North American Craton. Longer than that, it might be a place called Molten Blob of Magma. Some of these so-called "places" were good for mushrooms. Others – such as the ice shield and the molten blob – not so much.'

'We can time travel,' say the Martians. 'Which would be the best time slot for seeing a musical, in your opinion?'

'Maybe the Canada one,' says the mushroom. 'Present tense. Definitely not the Magma.'

'Okay, but what is it?' says the second Martian. 'The Canada one?'

'Many have asked,' says the mushroom. 'Some say it's a country.'

'But what is a country?' says the third Martian.

'Ah,' says the mushroom. 'You've heard of people?'

'Yeah, sure, of course,' says the first Martian. 'Two legs, only two arms, strange-looking heads, only two eyes. You need them for putting on musicals.'

'Okay, a country is an idea people get into their brains,' says the mushroom. 'Without people, there aren't any countries. Mushrooms don't bother with countries.'

'That's a start,' says the second Martian. 'What sort of idea, in their brains?'

'You draw a line, you put up walls and gates and such, you say some people can't come in and other people can't go out, you say everything inside this country is a certain kind of thing and that's how it is done inside the line you've drawn, you make laws, you have customs and a language, or two languages, or fifty-four languages, it depends. You have a flag, which is a piece of cloth with some sort of pattern on it, and it waves around in the wind. Unlike mushrooms: we don't wave anything. Maybe you have national outfits. You have a special song that you're supposed to sing, it's a ceremonial thing on special occasions. You're supposed to look really solemn and have deep emotions while doing it.'

'A song,' says the first Martian. 'That sounds promising, for musicals! At least it's a beginning.'

'What about dances?' says the second Martian. 'Musicals have dances. That's what the people need the legs for.'

'Some countries have national dances, others not,' says the mushroom. 'Sometimes the countries have wars. That's when they cross each other's lines and gates and so forth and try to kill the people in the other country so they can get all of their stuff, one way or another.'

'Stuff?'

'Toasters,' says the mushroom. 'Frying pans. Microwaves. All those anti-mushroom devices. Other stuff too, like land, gold, dead animals and trees. Fish – sometimes it's fish. I don't have much interest in fish myself, but some of these countries set a lot of store by them. Other countries are more interested in diamonds. But you can be obsessed by both.'

'Okay, so that's countries in general,' says the third Martian. 'What about this "Canada" country, then?'

'They value fish,' says the mushroom. 'Water on three sides. Large. A lot of mushrooms, though not so many as once. What else would you like to know?'

'From what you tell us,' says the first Martian, 'this "Canada" wasn't always there. Where did it come from?'

'Once upon a time,' says the mushroom, settling into narrative mode, 'the Laurentide Ice Sheet melted, and then there could be people. They had different languages. They were interested in fish, also animals. They had outfits and laws and customs and so forth, and songs. They had a lot of songs. But they didn't have this flag thing.'

'We don't either,' say the Martians.

'Maybe you'd better get one,' says the mushroom. 'They come in handy.'

'For what?' say the Martians.

'Claiming,' says the mushroom.

'I don't grasp your meaning,' says the first Martian. 'What is claiming?'

'In this specific instance,' says the *Amanita*, 'some people with a flag sailed over the ocean blue, and when they got to this side they stuck the flag in the ground – it was on a pole – and said, "I claim this land for France." Then they made a speech and wrote things down, and said the whole place was theirs, including all the fish, trees and animals, and the people who were already there. And the mushrooms. We mushrooms didn't get a say in it. Of course nobody pays any attention to us anyway, unless they eat a poisonous sporocarp.'

'What's a sporocarp?' says the second Martian.

'You're talking to one. So the people with the French flag set up a sort of sub-country, and had wars with some other people to the south who had done the same sort of claiming thing down there, but with a different flag.'

'I see what you mean about flags,' say the Martians. 'We should indeed concoct one for ourselves. But did they do musicals, these flag-waving people?'

'Thing about people,' says the mushroom, 'first they have wars. Then, after a while, they turn the wars into musicals. It's just how they are.'

'What about the people who were already there?' say the Martians. 'The ones without flags?'

'Things didn't go so well for them,' says the mushroom. 'To begin with, the new people were full of deadly spores. They didn't know it, but they were practically half poisonous mushroom. And their spores poisoned a lot of the people who were already there, and they died. With the ones who didn't die, things were sort of friendly at first, because the new people wanted animals. They wanted to put them on their heads, and also sell them to make lots of money. And the old people knew how to catch the animals. So things went on like that for a while.'

'On their heads?' ask the Martians. 'Why?'

'Don't ask me,' says the mushroom. 'They liked it, what can I say? Then there was a war between the French-flag ones and the English-flag ones to see who would control the dead animals, and the French-flag ones lost, and the English ones took over the dead-animal trade. Then after a while the animals got used up, and the English-flag ones thought that instead they would get people to grow wheat and make money out of that instead.'

'What is wheat?' say the Martians.

'It's anti-mushroom,' says the mushroom. 'Wheat pushed the mushrooms off a lot of land. You can't grow wheat and mushrooms in the same place and time. The original people got pushed off too, once they were no longer useful to the new people for catching the animals, for helping with the different wars, and for teaching the new people their knowledge about how to live here.'

'Those new people don't sound very grateful,' says the first Martian.

'That's how it is with people,' says the mushroom. 'If they want to take a thing that belongs to someone else, gratitude goes out the window. So the new people made laws about the first people, and the first ones didn't get a say. Things got bad for them. Plus a lot of poor people were shipped in, one way or another. Orphans, refugees, persecuted religions and whatnot. Many different languages, even more than at first! The ones shipped in were supposed to grow wheat. Things were bad for them too, because they were so poor, and didn't have thick winter coats. They had to eat parsnips. I think it was parsnips. And so it went on.

'Then after a while some of the higher-ups decided to call the place Canada – I forget which came first, the wheat or the name change – but it was still only a kind of sub-country. The big sporocarp was a king or a queen, who cares which – mushrooms don't do genders – who lived on the other side of the ocean.'

'I'm confused,' says the second Martian.

'I'm alarmed,' says the third Martian.

'I'm bored,' says the first Martian. 'Let's get to the musicals. What is *Canada: The Musical?*'

'There isn't one,' says the mushroom, 'because for the musicals you need to have a story. You need to decide how the story should come out – what's the finale? But in this Canada place, they've been arguing about the story for a lot of years. Is it the story of the French-language people and how they didn't do so well for a while? Is it the story of forging ahead with the wheat? There was something about a railroad too, but it's not very musical. Is it the story about welcoming new kinds of people, or is it the story about not welcoming new kinds of people, especially those with different coloured caps and scales? Canada, land of opportunity, or Canada, land of unfair discrimination and exploitation? You could do both.

'Is it the story about how one kind of sporocarp didn't have this thing called "the vote" at first, but then they got hold of it? Is it the story about how the first people here were shoved aside, and these other people made up laws about them and took their stuff, but now they're getting some of it back? There are a lot of stories, and all of them are true in their way, but not all of them would give you a rousing hurrah finale, plus dancing.'

'I can see it's a puzzle,' says the second Martian. 'Where to begin?'

'That's their problem, the Canada people,' says the mushroom. 'They don't know where to begin, and they don't know what to put in. Or what to leave out. No matter how you tell the Canada story, someone is going to be offended. Then they all say "Sorry" a lot.'

'They sound inhibited,' says the third Martian. 'Should we maybe just try to find New York? They have more *joie de vivre* there.'

'They used to have,' says the mushroom. 'Once upon a time. They did a million musicals; mostly stories about themselves. Or about cats. None of them bothered to tell the story about us mushrooms, though. Why isn't there *Mushrooms: The Musical*? There's a musical about everything else!'

'Mushrooms don't sing and dance, to be fair,' says the third Martian.

'That's no excuse,' says the *Amanita*, sulkily. 'Neither do lions, and look at *The Lion King*!'

'We're trying to,' say the Martians. 'We just don't know where it is. Where is this New York, where the musicals are?'

'It's south of here,' says the mushroom. 'Though I realize that's vague. But I think it's getting hostile to Martians down there. Safer for you here. Tell you what: why don't you make a flag, attach it to a pole, stick it into the ground, and claim Canada? Then you can be the ones who decide what should be in *Canada: The Musical*. Do me a favour – put in some mushrooms. *Amanita muscaria* is a melodious name for the heroine of a musical, don't you think?'

'That's a really good idea!' says the first Martian.

'Amanita, Amanita, how I loooove you,' croons the mushroom. 'Then there's a modern dance number, with a chorus dressed as decomposing vegetation . . .'

'I mean it's a good idea about the flag,' says the first Martian.

'And claiming Canada for the Martians,' says the second Martian. 'Then we can have musicals non-stop!'

'Let's do this!' says the third Martian. 'We can back it up with our sure-fire drone-controlled ray guns.'

And so they do. ∎

Karen Solie

A Sharing Economy

This performance of
'I Want My Fucking Money'
broadcast live from the street will conclude
when the last human being on earth
has perished.

The Freshly Renovated Bachelor Suite has its ear
to the ground, has the ear
of the Paying Guest
who's found a bed down there among
the learning experiences
and automatic functions,
decor objects from HomeSense's
Blunt Force Trauma Collection

above which the house hovers like a spaceship
in a super-convenient location
and the Hosts walk overland.

A pilot light flickers
like an awareness of self,
chaos whispering through the fittings,

pipes singing, patterns
in the textiles repeating, the weeping tile –

between sound and silence
is music.

The Paying Guest rises in the middle of the night
to turn off the radio where no radio exists,

a disturbance imminent over the sea – no
the lake –
it will come clear in a minute.

The furnace knocks twice
then hesitates, and the Paying Guest
lying in the lettings
remembers the old joke about the drummer
and now the Paying Guest is laughing on the inside.

THE BOOK TREE

Larry Tremblay

TRANSLATED FROM THE FRENCH BY SHEILA FISCHMAN

At a time so close at hand, God was everywhere and no one could murder Him.

It was spring but winter was hanging on. The roads were slippery. It was snowing, it was raining. It was bleeding, the car had hit a moose. The animal's blood was freezing on the windshield.

I came into the world amid my father's blasphemies on a country road. It was the first day of spring but winter hadn't said its last word. My mother was howling and breaking in two. My mother was giving birth in a Pontiac that had just killed a great creature of fur and antlers.

I made a hole in the newborn day. I did not know that questions existed. I opened my mouth to eat the time that was falling onto me.

One week later, snowdrops and tufts of dandelions were braving the sky above Rivière-du-Chagrin, 'River of Sorrow', where I, a bundle riddled with cries, made a hole in the world.

My father told me that he plunged me into the steaming body of the moose to warm me. And my mother, listening to him that day, smiled in her self-conscious silence. I asked why the river where I was born had a name filled with tears. And my mother told me that in the last century a young girl named Béatrice had hurled herself into it. People could hear the sobs of her stillborn child rise to the surface of the water. Ever since, the Rivière-du-Chagrin has been swollen with sorrow.

As for me, I was consumed by happiness at being a brand-new baby balanced on the world in his mother's arms.

Yes, I showed up before the spring thaw, on a road obstructed by the carcass of a moose.

I was baptized Joseph Ariel. Little by little I began to resemble my name. In starched white shirts, I memorized the commandments. Secretly I drank coffee to grow faster. I looked out from the living-room window at the cars becoming bigger. Their headlights read the fog.

I learned, head bowed, how to write, to count, to pray. I watched through the classroom window as the blue sky faded.

On the day I turned seven, my father gave me a watch, fastened it around my wrist.

Little by little I began to resemble my face. I knew the imperfect. I loved words, I put an 's' on them when they were numerous, I made verbs agree when they quarrelled. I dreamed of dictionaries. I crammed myself with liquorice, honeymoons, caramels. My baby teeth crumbled like sugar cubes. A dentist pulled seven at once, I counted my blood clots, I learned detachment.

I liked storms, the smell of earthworms, the terrifying forest. I fought with my friends, I liked to see their blood on the sidewalk. The sky over Rivière-du-Chagrin slipped into the gutters and weather fell onto my astonished eyelashes.

I recited the catechism, a foreign language that rang out in my skull like a bell in a storm.

At Christmas, under the tree, I surrounded Jesus with straw, I conversed with the ox, the ass, I stuck Joseph's plaster head back on.

I served at Mass. Sculpted into an altar boy, I helped the priest button his cassock. Along with him I sang the litanies in Latin, I lit the long church candles, I observed with disgust the kneeling adults waiting to receive the body of Christ, tongues extended like fish out of water.

I intuited everything that was rotting deep inside their bodies. To soothe my craving for the absolute, I munched, on the sly, sacramental bread in the sacristy. Because it was out of the question to digest the Son of God alongside last night's supper, I created, in my imagination a second stomach, impervious to corruption. My belly swollen with Christ, I walked like a cosmonaut, fearful that sanctified life would ooze through all the holes in my body. Floating in the mystery of flesh, my brain had no words to contribute.

Yet I loved words, I loved to gnaw on them before I knew what they meant, to mix them into my meals and sometimes swallow them whole like so many profane Hosts.

I imagined secret wars in my two stomachs. My mouth opened like a missal that dropped its versicles and its spittle onto the populace of Rivière-du-Chagrin.

I aspired to sainthood but there was no one in the area, not even in the next village, to crucify me and crown me with thorns. I defied the universe with my little fist: if there was God, there was the Devil. Who could prove to me that the one was not the other? I was given a choice between evil and good, it seemed like not much. Was there anything else? I scratched evil, found good. I scratched good, found evil.

My mother cast seven children into the world like a pack of cards onto a table. I was the eldest, the big brother, utterly unlike them. I gazed at the ancient tree in front of the house. I assumed that none of its leaves resembled the others. The maple, never identical to its shadow, was uncomplaining.

I spent a lot of time under my bed with the dust bunnies. I lay in wait for evil spells, I defied ghosts. I had a stomach ache. I felt dirty. I wanted to disappear. I broke the bulb of my face by making up questions. I sensed things that were stirring under my skin. I gave birth to weighty and appalling thoughts. Was someone other than me speaking inside me?

One night, when everyone was asleep, I decided to stop breathing. My bedroom wavered like a small boat. My skeleton became disarticulated, my body a sack. A hole as black as the one in the kitchen sink appeared in my consciousness. Would I escape myself like fluid down the drain? Leave nothing but the skin of a child that my mother, come morning, would sweep up with a broom?

When I breathed again I came to this conclusion: I had failed childhood, its train had departed without me. Alone on the platform, lost, I spied a display of books. I stole one. It was a novel of unhappy love and stupendous adventures. I was surprised that the story it told, so remote from my life, gave my life back to me even more alive.

I had overtaken the train that I'd missed. I'd been born again between the pages of an open book. Fiction challenged reality in a duel. Eyes burning, I was discovering literature. I fled with my paper flames into the branches of a tall pine where I built a cabin. Perched in my tree house I read, I read, my forehead as vast as the sky. I forgot my questions, Rivière-du-Chagrin forgot its sorrow and memory itself flowed towards the imaginary river. The maples around me were stripped bare but the tall pine kept its needles, reading over my shoulder. My fingers made blue by January trembled, turned chapters of fratricidal war that chilled my heart. I warmed myself with the fate of lovers who by way of farewell revelled in one final kiss before dying. I read, I read, my pupils starving, my soul opening like a gulf. I discovered the horror of happiness, the mud of lies, tired glories.

A book, brain open like a sky, road plunging into childhood.

Childhood, another name for infinity.

In my book tree, I imagined happy endings for tragic stories and for happy stories, harrowing endings. I turned pages and reality turned away from itself. I shook up life, indifferent to the pain I hoped to inflict. ■

© KARINE LAVAL
Poolscape #59, 2010

SWIMMING COACH

Anosh Irani

When his brother told him that he should read a short story by an American named John Cheever, Ulrich immediately thought of at least ten better ways to spend the evening. He could gather all the two- and five-rupee coins scattered in different corners of his room and go downstairs to the Irani restaurant and exchange them for paper currency. He could go to the laundromat across the street and finally collect his socks and underwear.

Or maybe he could just stay put. Why do anything? The smallest of his movements would add to the mayhem. Clare Road was a gaudy mix of hair salons, coffin makers, churches, cheap boutiques, and – worst of all – schools. Those screaming brats had managed to hijack Clare Road. Now everyone and everything had that unbearable quality that most children have.

'Just read the Cheever,' said Moses. His brother was still looking for the key to his motorcycle, which Ulrich knew was lying on the floor, at the foot of the table. 'This guy, this loser American rich type, he's at a pool party, and he suddenly decides to swim all the way home through people's backyards.'

'How the hell do you swim through a backyard?'

'Through their pools, yaar. He's tipsy and decides to go pool-hopping. But that's not what the story's *about* . . .'

'What do I care what it's about?'

'You're a swimmer so I just thought . . .'

Moses finally spotted the keychain. It was a terrible keychain for a motorcycle key. It had Moses's fiancée's name on it.

Ulrich pulled his white T-shirt all the way up to reveal his round belly. 'Do I look like a swimmer to you?' Ulrich slapped it hard, and it felt hard. That was the strange thing about his belly: it looked like fat but felt like muscle. But today it was extra firm – he hadn't been able to go the bathroom in two days. 'I'm a coach, man,' said Ulrich. 'Very different from a swimmer. Swimmers swim, coaches sit and watch.'

'Then just sit there for the rest of your life. Just sit there and stare out the window.'

'Why does it bother you so much?'

'Because that's all you do. It's embarrassing.'

'So is your fucking keychain.'

Cussing always got to Moses. His brother had always been the more mannered of the two, the darling pupil at school, whereas Ulrich's brain retained nothing; every single line that he read passed through the way hot chai passes through a strainer. The only thing Ulrich excelled at was sport.

'I'll be back late,' said Moses.

'So why you telling me? I'm not your mother.'

Ulrich regretted saying that. Moses kept trying to bridge the distance between them by simple gestures; today, it was by asking Ulrich to read a story. That way, the brothers would have something to talk about at night.

From the veranda, Ulrich stared out at Monginis, the cake shop opposite. He envisioned his mother buying sponge cakes. He could still see her, eight years after her death, wiping the edges of her mouth with her small white handkerchief, two dabs on the left and two dabs on the right. It was as though the white handkerchief and the dabbing ensured that nothing cruel ever came out of her mouth. Unlike his mouth.

Below, Moses was wiping the seat of his RX 100. Why did he have to wipe the seat five times? It was not a baby's bottom. It was a goddamn bike. Ulrich fought the urge to spit on it.

A year ago, he would have done it. At thirty-nine, spitting would have made sense. But turning forty changed things. He had lost almost all of his hair, except for a meaningless tuft, an apologetic afterthought, at the back of his head, for which he still had to pay barbers' fees. He was now a man with a moustache, a look he had always despised.

As he walked back into the living room, he saw the book by John Cheever lying on the sofa. What the hell, he thought. Cheever's company in the bathroom might do his bowels some royal good.

He read the story through and through, but he did not know what to make of it. There was a distinct tempo and each time he thought of closing the book, he found himself turning the page instead. His belly was now empty and clean, but his mind was running. He could not understand why the man, after completing a marathon swim through countless private pools (and a noisy public one), and even crossing a highway on foot, had to stand outside his own home, which was locked, and peer into it through the window, thinking his wife was waiting for him when the home was empty and deserted.

But this was not the question that was really burning him.

What the fuck was Moses trying to tell him? From the time his brother left, two hours ago, Ulrich had guzzled five beers. He was tipsy now too, like Cheever's swimmer. Had his brother finally learned to fight, to spit back? Suddenly, Ulrich was all charged up. He circled the flat, a man on the verge of an important discovery. But when nothing came, and there was only the lazy grey of dusk to contend with, he had a sixth beer and went to sleep.

An hour later, he woke up with a start. He sprung out of bed with the liveliness of a sudden hard-on and rushed to the mirror. 'I'm Ulrich,' he shouted. That bastard is messing with me, he thought. I'll show him.

Ulrich was a distinctive name. Even in the Catholic community in Bombay – the 'Macs' as they were affectionately called – he knew no one who shared his name. His mother had named him after St Ulrich, and when he said his name out loud, as he had done now, it felt even more German. Germans were tough. They did not shy away from confrontation. Germany was his favourite football team. The players had the precision of machines, of machines that could produce sweat and were made of blood. As a swimmer, one had to be the perfect combination of human and machine. That was his belief.

He found himself perspiring even though the ceiling fan above him was at full zoom. He took off his T-shirt and threw it on the bed. It wasn't enough. He took his shorts off too and stood stark naked before the mirror. Then, in a sudden fit, he put his Speedos on, stuffed some money in them, grabbed his swimming goggles and walked out the door.

On his way down the stairs, he passed his next-door neighbour, Sunita, who let out a shriek. Or maybe it was a squeal. Her husband was a scrawny man with toothpicks for legs. Ulrich had done her a favour by showing off his muscular thighs.

With an air of confidence, he stepped out into the street.

It did not matter that people were staring at him. What did these morons know anyway? Cheever's swimmer had the advantage of plush pools and soft lawns and the occasional fancy drink to help him along his journey. Cheever's swimmer did not have to contend with the mocking stares of the Bombaywala. When a Bombaywala showed disapproval, you felt it in the very marrow of your being. Tonight Ulrich would use those waves of disapproval to build muscle.

The hot shop lights along the footpath made his dark skin shine, and he took a left towards the fire station. Soon he was walking through Madanpura, a cocoon for the underworld, known for its contract killers and loan sharks. Yet the darkness of the streets was soothing. If he were to walk here in broad daylight, he'd be sure to get a nice tight slap from someone. But now everyone was busy buying sweets or getting their beard shaved. It was only near the Salvation Army that a lady in a burka gasped at him. He did not falter but hurried on towards the YMCA.

'I lost my keys,' he told the man at reception and walked past him.

'But coach . . .' said the man, leaping up to follow him, whispering that he needed to cover himself.

'Just chill, yaar,' said Ulrich. 'I'm doing only one lap.'

'Laps? But I thought you lost your keys.'

'I lost them in the pool, man.'

He dove in with perfect technique. When his large belly hit the water, it just slid in naturally, along with the rest of him, with minimum fuss. In his enthusiasm, he forgot to remove his rubber chappals and the money that was tucked into his Speedos. The chappals he let go of after the first few strokes. They rose to the surface and stayed there, lolling about, as Ulrich reached the other end. The goggles followed. Just like Cheever's swimmer, he refused to use the ladder to get out of the pool.

He remembered the fat kid that he had trained that very morning and how upset he'd been when the kid struggled to get out of the pool even *with* the use of the ladder. It was pathetic how this kid's pudgy arms had no strength; full of milk and butter and biscuits, his body did not deserve to be in the pool. 'What will help my son?' the kid's mother asked Ulrich after the private training session.

'Iraq,' Ulrich had wanted to reply.

Dripping wet and sufficiently chlorinated, he coolly walked towards the exit near the kitchen. The canteen owner greeted Ulrich nonchalantly, but then his expression changed to one of bewilderment.

'What the hell are you doing?' he asked.

'I'm broke,' said Ulrich. 'Have to walk around in my *chaddis*. Tell the committee what a state I'm in.'

Outside, stray dogs were tearing apart a piece of rotten meat the butcher had thrown their way. Ulrich slid into the back seat of a taxi despite the driver's protests.

'I'll give you seven hundred rupees,' said Ulrich, thrusting his hand inside his Speedos and withdrawing a wet bundle of shrunken notes. 'I want to go to Marine Drive, with two stops in between. That's all.' Ulrich spread out all the money he had on the back seat, assuring the driver that none of the notes were torn. Once he saw that the driver was satisfied, he handed him the cash. The driver put it in the glove compartment and took off.

The stale wind hit Ulrich's chest and sent a shiver through him so he rolled up the windows even though the air was hot. The first stop was outside a newly constructed building at Saat Rasta.

Ulrich walked up to the security guard and told him to let Tony know that he was here.

Tony was the only school friend Ulrich had kept over the years. He was now the creative director of one of the biggest ad agencies in the city. All those long-haired, goateed *lunds* who walked around pretending they were geniuses, when all they did was come up with a byline for soap. It pissed him off, it really did, but it pissed him off even more that he did not have a single creative bone in his entire body.

'Boss, what's wrong with you?' Tony asked. 'You smashed or what?'

'I need to use your pool.'

'My pool?'

'Ya, men. It's urgent.'

'The pool's closed,' said Tony. 'They had some issue . . .'

'Fuck,' said Ulrich.

'Are you okay? Coming here in trunks and all . . .'

'All okay, men. All good. But I need a favour,' said Ulrich.

'Sure, men,' said Tony. 'Anything.'

'I need to swim at the Willingdon. Can you get me in?'

'Willingdon? No chance! Even *I'm* not a member. Those *chaunts* don't take any new members only. Even if you have the cash.'

The Royal Willingdon Sports Club was the city's most elite club, with a pool surrounded by bougainvillea and coconut trees Ulrich had never swum in it. He'd only seen it up close once when he applied for the job of swimming coach five years ago. He thought he had nailed it but then the hiring committee asked to watch him interact with the members' children, to see how effective he was as a coach. He knew he was screwed. Not because he was a bad coach – far from it. He was a terrific coach, but from the pool he had looked up and caught the eye of one of the members who lived near the YMCA. The member recognized Ulrich as the same sick man who had shown *Jaws* to young boys at summer camp, for training purposes. Ulrich had told them that if they could watch *Jaws* and *then* get into the pool that very instant, they would be able to swim anywhere. All of them jumped into the pool immediately after the film, with real gusto, except for one kid, who ended up making an unnecessary fuss, and rushed out to call his mother. No one at the YMCA cared much about the incident; in fact it had garnered Ulrich some accolades from old-timers who felt that kids nowadays had it too easy and needed some mental discipline. And even though Ulrich was doing a terrific job of interacting with his pretend students at the Willingdon, the member grinned through his teeth, and Ulrich could feel this old shark catching up with him, nibbling away at his ankles, then his knees, and then, the final gash in the thigh, in the form of a polite 'no' when he called the next day to ask if he had gotten the job.

'But why you need to swim *now*?' asked Tony.

'I have to,' said Ulrich. 'I just have to.' Then he put his hand on Tony's shoulder, looked him straight in the eye and said, 'Will you help me?'

'I'll get you another pool.'

'No. It has to be the Willingdon.'

'Why?'

'Because it's on the way.'

'To where?'

Ulrich did not answer. He just mumbled something about Tony being the best friend he ever had and forced him into the taxi. On the way to the Willingdon, Ulrich slapped Tony's thigh. 'What times we've had,' he said and looked out the window. He was wistful, and when he adjusted himself in the back seat, his wet naked back made a squishy sound against the Rexine, like some small animal being squashed against the wall of a cage.

They asked the driver to wait in the parking lot. It was dark now and the two men stayed close to the bushes. It would be impossible for anyone to enter the Willingdon through the main entrance, but the pool entrance was separate and the only obstacle was the man at the reception desk who handed out towels and placed your wristwatch in a drawer. Tony's job was to distract him, which he did by telling him that a stray dog was running amuck in the gentlemen's dressing room. It was easy to believe because stray dogs did walk the lawns of the club from time to time, enjoying leftover sandwiches that patrons fed them from the leisure of their cane chairs.

As soon as Tony led the man into the gents' change room, Ulrich entered through the white gate that was more like a pretty picket fence. He picked up a fresh towel, slung it around his shoulder and scanned the pool. There were only three people in it: an old man who lay sprawled on the descending steps like some raja with his eyes to the heavens, his tummy partly outside the water, forming a half watermelon; a woman who was conscientiously doing laps, but her technique was all wrong – the way she stuck her head out of the water would surely lead to a neck injury at some point; and a teenager, his muscles rippling with stupidity.

Ulrich threw the towel aside and took a couple of deep breaths. He had come to the realm of the rich and successful, men and women who rang a small bell to summon the waiter, and ordered kejriwal on toast – just egg and cheese, but when they ordered it, it had weight and taste – and when stray cats rubbed against their leather shoes they threw scraps of food towards them, the same way life had thrown scraps of luck towards Ulrich, causing him to jump into the air for more, like a circus animal, only to bite into thin air.

Swimming at the Willingdon, as a member, as he was about to do right now, would give him the illusion of success, a temporary confidence and strength that would help him face these people.

He expanded his chest and dove.

The first lap was purely functional, to get the arms and legs moving again, and get the body adjusted to the pool temperature, which was nice and warm. Once he had his breathing right, which occurred during the second lap, he felt he was on autopilot, and that was the trick, to conserve energy, and during the third lap, he forgot about energy completely, took his mind out of the equation the way yogis discard all thought during meditation but retain a simple and humble awareness.

The pool lights were on. They provided a gentle glow from beneath which reminded him of something – of early mornings spent with his mother as dawn came, so softly, treating all humans like babies, all Earth creatures like fragile, magical beings who needed whispering and encouragement. But the water was too sharp, too chlorinated for him to keep his eyes open. He closed them, his body settling into an easy rhythm the way the heart settles at the onset of an afternoon siesta, that beautiful sinking feeling of falling *through* the mattress; even though he was on the surface of the water, in a sense he was going deeper, and he made a perfect turn when he hit the other end, his body curling into a foetus, then gracefully springing to life, moving towards the other side with new-born energy. He was at home in the water, and it was from here that he would find ways to live, reasons to live, and he suddenly went deeper, cut across the pool, as though he had spotted an old acquaintance at a marketplace or among a crowd of strangers. No one could see him here, no human eyes could touch him, and he felt secure, un-judged, happy to pull in a modest salary, have enough money to buy the occasional pair of jeans or a round of drinks for a friend or two. Here, inside, it was warm and kind, and he came to the surface not because he needed air, but because he had gotten something that he could take with him to his final visit. It was not what he had expected; he had expected something electric, but he ended up imbibing a soft light instead, which was so much better. He stepped out of the pool, wrapped the towel around his waist and left. Tony would be okay to take a different cab back home.

This time Ulrich rolled the window down. As the taxi took a left turn at Wilson College, he stuck his chest out and let the wind from the Arabian Sea bring its salt to him. At Wilson, Ulrich had been one of the cool ones, smoking joints, wearing jeans that he had rubbed for hours with sandpaper to give the area near the thighs an almost-torn look, and while others studied history and literature, he gave drug-induced sermons on why 'Comfortably Numb' by Pink Floyd was one of the greatest songs ever written, and how music could get you in an instant, it was the heroin of life, whereas books took their own sweet time and hardly gave you a lift, which was why even though he was an arts student he refused to read. It was at one such free-falling campus lecture – delivered under a large banyan tree to about four or five regular stoners – that he managed to impress Angela, the hottest Catholic girl at college. He liked that she did not put any powder on her face to make her skin lighter. She had a dark radiance to her, an inner fuck-you shine that resonated with Ulrich. She was like Ulrich, he felt, but she had a brain. So while she was talking to her friend, he took her copy of Chaucer, tore out a couple of pages, put some weed in them and tried to smoke it. 'It's useless,' he said to her. 'But if you and I smoke a large healthy bugger and listen to Floyd, we'll be flying.' She liked his guts, but that was much later, about a year after she slapped him.

Now, as the taxi took the stretch towards Marine Drive, he longed to be that age again, to smoke joints and bite Angie's dark juicy Christian thighs over long summer days and nights. But they were both forty now, and in different worlds. He was suddenly hungry, for food, but then the very thought of eating anything put him off. Perhaps he was just nervous.

'Boss,' he told the taxi driver. 'Just stop here.'

He looked at the taxi driver and smiled – it was the smile of
a man who was thankful and defeated at the same time. The taxi
driver just nodded and drove away. By morning the notes in the glove
compartment would dry up and have the strange crispy shape of
silver foil.

He climbed up the steps to one of the ground-floor apartments
and rang the bell. The door opened almost immediately, which he
certainly wasn't ready for, at all.

'Angie . . .' he said. 'I . . .'

She looked like she had put on some weight, and that made him
happy. She had lost some juice; there was no doubt about it.

'Ulrich?' she said. 'What are you . . . you know you can't come
here.'

'I know, I know. But I just wanted to see you.'

It seemed not to matter to Angela that Ulrich was wearing only
a towel. The very fact that he had shown up seemed to bother her and
he could sense that.

'How's . . .'

'She's not here,' said Angela.

Ulrich felt relieved when she said that. It had been seven years
since he had seen them both, and even if he saw his daughter this very
instant he would not know that she was his because a baby can grow
into anything, there are hundreds of permutations and combinations.
The current man in her life, the man who owned this expensive
apartment on Marine Drive, who was a Willingdon member, had
once been Ulrich's friend, and Angela had borrowed money from
him for her dental work, without asking Ulrich, and it had hurt him
deeply, so deeply that he had slapped Angie, and beat the shit out
of his friend, and it was soon after his mother's death, and he was
so raw that he eventually drove them into each other's arms. It was
such a stupid reason for the end of a marriage. A slap had started
their relationship and a slap had ended it as well. But perhaps Angie
was not who he had thought she was. She chose money over love.
The reality of spending the rest of her life in one room, in a small flat

on Clare Road which Ulrich shared with his brother, was too much for her. The divorce was swift and the deal sweet: his friend, whom Ulrich had beaten up because he thought the two were having an affair, would not press charges if he gave Angie full custody.

But it was not the threat of criminal action that scared him. He signed his name in disgust on that sheet of paper because he knew he would never be able to provide for them the way he wanted to. The signature was the clearest signature anyone could ever make, as clear as his self-loathing.

'I'm sorry,' he said to Angela. 'I shouldn't have come.'

Here he was, apologizing once again. He saw how Angela leaned against the door, half her body shielded behind it, as if he were a trespasser or common criminal. Slowly, she was closing the door, inch by inch, and just before she did, she looked into his eyes, and he felt a tiny shiver until the sound of the door closing coincided with a stiff ocean breeze hitting the side of his neck and stomach. He suddenly felt very exposed.

He waited for the light to turn red and quickly crossed the road to the huge black expanse of the Arabian Sea. He wrapped the towel around him like a shawl and stood on the parapet. Below, large grey boulders separated the water from him. During the monsoons, the water levels rose so high the boulders were submerged and the waves lashed the shore relentlessly, until the fissures tore at the walls and made them crumble.

It was one big swimming pool out there, and if he swam in a straight line he would reach the Gulf of Aden and enter Oman or Yemen, far away from Angela and his daughter, where he could earn much more as a swimming coach. Around him, the promenade was littered with lovers, holding hands and cooing promises to each other in the same way he and Angie once had. He slowly lowered himself onto the boulders, and in doing so, lost his towel. It didn't matter. Paper cones were strewn across the boulders and a few plastic bags floated in the wind. To his right, the skyline of the city glittered, the lights in skyscrapers burning passionately, the stars above less electric, less powerful. Tomorrow was Sunday. It was a working day for Ulrich. While the rest of the city read the morning papers, he would instruct a new batch of swimmers.

Perhaps, before going to work, he would wake Moses and tell him what he thought. That Cheever's swimmer was not mad to look into his own house through a window. He was looking at his past, trying to make sense of it, as all humans do, the way Ulrich had just done, and perhaps Ulrich was luckier than the swimmer because Ulrich knew where Angela was. She wasn't his anymore, nor was his child, but at least he knew where they lived.

Cheever's swimmer, it seemed, had come to the terrible realization that he would never see his family ever again. Ulrich also wanted to tell Moses the real ending of the story. Way after Cheever's story ended, the swimmer went around the house to the pool, to his very own pool, where the water was green and slimy, and he slid in, without technique, without grace, just a body slipping into nature, the chlorine and algae and bacteria touching his skin, causing a chemical reaction, changing him, working his brain, dissolving all its memories, one after another, the way acid works on something, moments shared with his wife and daughter turning into nothing, or perhaps returning to the water, to nature itself, as nature had always intended, and the swimmer, always a mammal, shrinking, collapsing, exhaling, inhaling, and sighing a final breath of relief as the world turned another day. ■

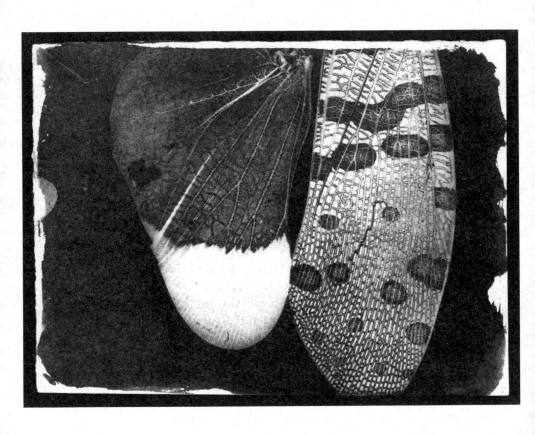

OF ROSES AND INSECTS

Chloé Savoie-Bernard

TRANSLATED FROM THE FRENCH BY NEIL SMITH

He wants to drive me to my dad's, but I tell him to drop me off at the subway. I'll take the bus alone. In the car, he makes jokes, talks about my dad, says Joël this and Joël that, and I half laugh. In our conversations, Joël is a character in a book, a puppet on a string. One of the first things I ever told him was that I have daddy issues. Talk, talk, talk as he parks. Then he puts his hand on my thigh, draws it up my side, brushes against my breasts, grips my windpipe, but gently. I feel reassured, as though he's checking that all my organs are where they should be, as he sticks his tongue in my mouth, puts his hand on my throat. Anyway, you don't need to breathe when you kiss. We've been together for almost three years and I haven't introduced him to my dad. Nothing seems more offensive, strange, inappropriate than the image of those two sitting together at the family dinner table, their love for me juxtaposed.

As usual when I catch the 141 bus at Saint-Michel subway station and see the ugliness of Jean Talon Street all the way to Pie-IX Boulevard, I feel the anxiety building beneath my skin. Little grey insects flutter up my oesophagus, hover in my throat. Everything my boyfriend has just sealed inside me – my heart, my lungs, the veins carrying my blood – suddenly cracks open, comes undone, and my body is crawling with beetles and dragonflies. I feel them burrowing through my dermis, bumping against the top layer of my skin, growing angry, stinging me on the inside. Prick, prick, prick.

When I arrive at his house, my dad, as usual, thanks me ad nauseam for coming. Honey, he calls me. Sweetheart. His bloodshot eyes go teary. He glides his hand up my arm, rubs my shoulder a few seconds in the front hall while I still have my coat on.

It burns wherever he touches me.

My sister turns up a minute later. I don't see you two enough, my dad says, I miss you. He always says, My children, my darlings, you are my life. On the phone, he'll usually add, A father's love for his daughters is unique. He says he loves his sons, but what he feels for my sister and me is special, different. When my brothers are around, he'll never claim he loves his daughters any differently. He'll say, I love all four of you, equally. Sometimes, he'll say, I love all five of you. The fifth child he refers to was in fact never born: my mom miscarried the first time she was pregnant.

Today, he wonders aloud, Did I have any other children? More than four? More than five? He doesn't mean half-brothers or half-sisters I might have somewhere, illegitimate children he had with other women. What he implies is that he believes my mom had abortions without telling him. My dad divides his offspring into the living and the dead – real and imaginary ghosts. He says, Children are a treasure.

That he wishes he had a dozen.

We kids, his living children, say nothing in response. Buzz, buzz, buzz goes the scarab as it kisses the glow-worm in my mouth.

Unlike my sister and me, who escaped long ago, my two brothers still live at home and seldom go out. Inhabiting this house is their only activity, the only use of their time. They're not well and never have been: together they've amassed an impressive number of psychiatric diagnoses. Today we all sit around the table, nobody talking much.

In my dad's house, the only shiny new thing is the white kitchen, which looks suburban, bourgeois, flashy. It was recently renovated and not a kitchen I would have chosen because it just emphasizes the awful state the other rooms are in. The rest of the house has stayed as it was when my mom lived here. He calls her 'that woman', refusing to call her by her name. Other than the kitchen, nothing has really changed here since I was a kid, though everything looks more beat-up and run-down. Grungier. My dad asks how we're doing, my sister and I. What's new, girls? he says. I'm busy, I say, I'm working a lot. My dad is misty-eyed, his fingernails yellow and too long, and when I look at him, the insects wriggle in my throat. He says he's so happy I'm with someone. You could be with anybody, he tells me, the important thing is not to be alone.

Today is Father's Day, and as we've done every year since my parents divorced, my sister and I have bought our dad flowers. We give him four red roses, one from her, one from me, and two from our brothers, who never buy gifts, which is no big deal since we're used to it. We know they'll do nothing to mark the day, that it's up to us to find time to pick up gifts. That it's up to us to pay. There's still no vase in the house, and my dad apologizes. I forgot to buy one again, he says. He also apologizes for the mess – the yellow foam sticking out of the threadbare chairs, the cracks in the ceiling, the mouldy dishrags lying across the counters, the peeling wallpaper, the grimy windows – as I'm throwing out a jar of pink hair dye left on a shelf of the cabinet in the dining room. I used that dye ages ago, so I don't understand what this long-forgotten jar is doing there, and my dad doesn't either. I remember that back when I was fourteen, fifteen, sixteen, I'd dye my hair different colours – blonde, red, pink, green – hoping I'd undergo some profound change, but my head remained where it always was atop my neck and shoulders and I was still my parents' daughter. My father's daughter. It's when I spot the jar of hair dye that the insects move up to my eyes. They lay their lacy, veined wings like a lens over my pupils, and the room divides into segments. The insects dissect the layers of my father's life, our lives and my mother's life that have collected in this sad house. Layers like these usually speak volumes, reveal secrets when you dig through the different eras, but here, they have no depth; they lie parallel to each other. Cheap, shoddy artefacts.

As usual, we can't decide what to put the flowers in. The empty yogurt containers aren't deep enough, the drinking glasses not wide enough. We settle on an old champagne bucket sitting dirty in the middle of the living room. The last time champagne was uncorked in this house was probably twenty years ago when my dad defended his PhD. My dad rinses the bucket, places the flowers in it, wipes away a tear. I love you, he tells us again, I'm happy we're all here. Then he goes out for a smoke on the back patio. Beer bottles are hidden all over the yard, so maybe he'll have a drink too. If he's feeling especially brazen today, he'll pour himself some wine later. Will we say anything? It depends: sometimes we get tired of telling him he can't mix his meds and alcohol. If he drinks too much, he'll have a seizure or two, my brothers will pick him up off the floor, but my sister and I will already be gone. If they're minor attacks, Ariane and I will find out two or three weeks later, or maybe never. If they're serious, the hospital has our phone numbers. My sister and I are at the top of his call list.

While my dad is outside, my older brother says, For a vase, we should have gone to Dad's room, unlocked his door, and collected the empty beer bottles lying around. He says, We could have used one bottle for each rose, one bottle per kid. He laughs to himself and my sister and I look away. When my dad comes back in, my brother stops laughing, his face as stiff as a marionette's. The patio door isn't very thick. Can my dad hear us when he's outside? We wolf down our sushi, my sister barely speaking, me not saying a thing. My dad serves himself some wine, one glass, two glasses, three glasses, and after that I stop counting. My brothers chat about the weather and politics. Then my dad takes out four envelopes, solemnly. The envelopes look new, and he hands one to each of us. I unseal mine. His will is inside. My health's not so good any more, he tells us, I need to take precautions. He says, I don't want that woman to steal everything after I'm gone. He's left us each an equal share of his house.

I say, I don't want your house.

And for once, the insects keep quiet.

My sister laughs nervously. Anyway, happy Father's Day, she mutters. Then no one says a word. I stand up and so does my sister. As we're getting ready to go, my dad takes us in his arms, first me and then my sister. He gets weepy again. I love you, he tells us, I love you so much. He asks me, Will I meet your boyfriend soon? I realize my dad doesn't know his name, that I've never told him.

I catch the 141 in the opposite direction. My boyfriend is waiting for me at Saint-Michel station. How did it go at your father's? he asks. Same old, same old, I say. He kisses me, but the anxiety I felt on the way to my dad's place has lingered and created layers in my blood, depthless layers lined up side by side. His will is still in my handbag, and I don't know what I'll do with it. Its after-image seems to radiate through my bag, extending my dad's reach, burning my side. My boyfriend kisses me again, brushes against my hips. This time, he doesn't touch my throat, and I wonder if the insects living in my mouth have built nests in my mucous membrane, if their offspring are now hatching, if they'll soon be crawling along the walls of my windpipe. I wonder if while we're kissing, they're crossing from my pharynx to his.

I wonder if I'm infecting him. ■

© JULIE COCKBURN
First Flush, 2017
Hand embroidery on found photograph, Courtesy of Flowers Gallery

BINA

Anakana Schofield

Warning

I DO SWEAR.
IN THIS PLACE.
YOU WILL FIND.
WARNINGS.
IF YOU HEED THEM
THEY WILL BE YOURS.
IF YOU DON'T
YOU WERE WARNED.

My name is Bina and I'm a very busy woman. That's Bye-na not Beena. I don't know who Beena is, but I expect she's having a happy life. I don't know who you are, or the state of your life. But if you've come all this way here to listen to me, your life will undoubtedly get worse. I'm here to warn you, not to reassure you.[1]

I am a modern woman with modern thoughts on modern things. I'm not a young person so I am used to being ignored. I expect you won't listen. The last time we met nobody listened to me.

---

[1] Because I was reassured. He's a nice lad they said. He wasn't.

If you see me on the road and I pay no heed to you, know I have very good reasons for doing so. If you ever see a person lying in a ditch, drive straight past them as fast as you can. And if a man comes to your door, do not open it.

These serve as my first two warnings.
No ditch.
No door.

Do exactly as I tell you in matters mentioned.
I have lived to tell this tale.
You could be a lot less lucky.

Eddie is gone.

There is the Son of God the way there is the son of Bina.
His name is Eddie.

Eddie is a man.
Except Eddie is not Bina's real son.
He's her sorta son.
He managed to adopt himself onto Bina because she left her coat undone & in he climbed.
Latched + snatched.
That's Eddie.

Eddie's the kind of son you are landed with because no beggar wants to be bothered with him, and because he's used up all his goodwill and will soon expire on yours.

Eddie is gone.
We give thanks that
Eddie is gone.
We give thanks to God for that.

I didn't want him.

I didn't want to help him, but he presented in a manner that was impossible to ignore. Before I knew what I know now. Now I wouldn't help him. I won't help anyone. Not even you.

I'm only telling you this to warn you. I've better ways to waste my time than mithering on here. I'm a busy woman. Of that be certain. People think old women have nothing to do but stand around. They're very wrong and very ignorant and do take that last combination of wrong and ignorant as another warning. If people think you have time to stand about, let them know otherwise by not standing about. Take off! Take off when they least expect it. Could you just hold this for a minute? Don't! Be gone. Would you like to? No I wouldn't. Can I borrow your bread knife to take on a picnic? No. You can't. Because you'll never bring it back. Would there be any chance . . . ? No! There's no chance. None. None. None.

I will take exactly the time needed to tell my story & then it will stop. Any interruption or extension will not be my doing. It will be the infiltrators' or undertakers' or solicitors'; whomever finds this and whoever it is decides on these things. Don't trust a word said after I've stopped. The final full stop will be in red. That's how you'll know.

Don't arrive at the end of this tale insisting it was too long or too wide or too unlike you. I am not interested in appealing to you. I am not you. I am only here to warn you.

We are all here because of legal reasons we probably cannot articulate without getting in trouble, but we will not burden each other by staying a page longer than is necessary. And there should not be a page more than absolutely required. And if there is, write away and complain. There's probably an address to be found or a phone number. I won't care. Phone them all night long if you must. More likely you'll find a page missing. A page someone will have scratched out sentences or names in a thick black stripe. I'd better get going here fast before it happens.

Don't sign petitions for me. You might see them around. I have heard about them. Ignore them. Read this instead. You don't need 32,000 signatures to tell you anything as simple as what I am going to tell you here. Yes I was wronged, but I was serviceably wronged because I have been handed this undertaking. I am a practical woman, there's nothing I like more than to be useful and this makes me useful. This undertaking serves only as a warning to you, if you are thinking of opening your hearth or your heart. Don't. Of course I have better things to do like making lists and learning hymns. I hate hymns but it's important now not to stick out around here. If I stick out, I'll be lifted all over again and all will be more terrible than it already is and was and might ever be. No one in a choir gets arrested. No one suspects people in choirs. Everyone's in a choir. That's why there's no one in jail any more.
Think slow and careful on that.

She found him in a ditch.
It was very annoying.
Quite the interruption.
Especially for a Tuesday.
That was the first fella.
The young fella.
Eddie.

There are going to be two fellas Bina will warn you about.
Eddie's the first.
But the other fella.
There was another fella.
Isn't there always another fella?
Where there's one, there's two.
He came to the door.

Civilized
On a Tuesday
Worry about the civilized types
On Tuesdays.

Ask yourself if someone highly clean & civilized is standing at your
door, ask yourself what bold mischief that person could be capable
of, then imagine it twice as bad. Imagine them taking a sword and
lopping off your head. Then dragging a large knife down the front of
you, opening you up like a shirt and spilling your giblets out on the
path and rummaging through them. I generally find since I started
doing this, it prompts me to shut my door as swift as I open it.

If the sword isn't working and your door is still open, imagine them
taking a gun, a hunting rifle, the sort used to obliterate Bugs Bunny
and see yourself flung back against your airing cupboard peppered
with fat bullets. This is what some fellas like to do to women. Don't
let yourself be one of them.

Actually I'll put it direct: if they are knocking worry, worry about
them. They are all after something. It might be something you do or
don't have or are or aren't able for, but they can persuade you *they*
are ready for it and so *you've* to be ready. Heed me on this. Hear me.
I've made every mistake you've yet to make and, if you're intent on
not listening, are *about* to make.

And another thing, if someone asks you to put a bag over their head.
Don't do it.
They can change their mind.
That's what happened him.
The Tall Man.
Someone changed her mind.
A certain someone.
I can't name.

Because of the courts.
In Castlebar.
I shouldn't have named the place, but now I've no time to rub it out.
I have to carry on.
I'll have to give the tall man a name.
I'll call him Tall Man.
I'll call him Tall Man because I am in a hurry.
And because Kettle Man sounds a bit funny.
I am in a hurry because in case you didn't catch it earlier
I am a very busy woman.
If I write it out this way, in these stacks, you'll know I'm particularly in a hurry as I'm writing this bit.
I'll need you to hear it fast and roll up these papers if they are in your palm, or if anyone comes unexpectedly into the room. Just shut down the screen.
Someone is coming now so I'm going to shut it. Snap.

I'm back but I've forgotten where I was.
I'm in a hurry so I'll just carry on. I can't look back up there and my memory is not great so you may have to just read a few things twice. What harm? Nothing can be done about it. Nothing to be done. It's how it is when you are in a hurry.
I've just to go on until I am no longer or we'll never reach the red dot.

There's a thing about Eddie.
The thing about Eddie is he left.
The thing about Eddie is he's gone.
Everything about Eddie improved once he was gone.
That was the thing about Eddie.

There are a few more things about Eddie, but we'll get to them yet.
If we have time.
If we've no time
You'll have to make do with what's above. ∎

Daphne Marlatt

verbal pathways

from muddy streams to boulder creeks or water snakes
to water skaters flame trees weeping willow Brook to
Windsor we didn't escape the English reach of the
proper name

(retained by definition

from granite Flagstaff Hill to granite Grouse through green
time tunnel of angsana's golden bloom to Douglas fir dark
sentinels a boulevard a bouleversement

(open memory's closed roads . . . and what was home?

meranti's silver crown now cedar bough it's bush it's rain
forest wet the same but different *air* not air in streams
down slopes here gravelled water not the same

(a split blocks recognition

here on Hawks by Union bike-crossing summer slender
tree lifts hair-like fluff to crest this could be pink could be
some kind of pukul rain here yes a

rain tree shower

LIFE OF THE FATHER

Alain Farah

TRANSLATED FROM THE FRENCH BY LAZER LEDERHENDLER

1

S hafik Elias looks up, as though about to conclude. He scans the
room, his gaze gliding over the faces, some of them familiar,
others not. The silence is total, intense, almost liturgical; the
anticipation at its peak, the kind that comes before the punchline of
a good joke. Shafik leans towards the mike. Holding on to the lectern
with his fingertips, he takes a deep breath. 'I would be remiss if I did
not quote the words my father so often repeated to me: *Al-dunya fani
wa azzaman kabas.* Yes, my friends, let us enjoy this lovely evening,
for the life in which we are submerged is a trap, a trap contained in
the prison of time.'

Shafik takes a step back. The quality of the silence changes. For
a long second, people seem to hesitate. Then Shafik smiles, and the
applause erupts, instantly filling the entire hall, from the top tables to
the back of the mezzanine. The peroration of the speech has released
a peculiar energy among the hundred or so guests seated throughout
the two floors of La Toundra.

Eyes aglow with emotion, a proud smile playing on his lips,
Shafik absorbs the unmistakable electricity generated by applause.
He steps down from the dais, beyond which the river, the downtown

skyscrapers, the silhouette of the mountain, perhaps even the cross at its summit, are visible. A waiter walks between the top tables and the dais to make sure the guests are enjoying the long-awaited first course.

A woman at a table in the second row – let's call her Ruby Brume – wears a glimmering red satin dress and a look of perennial astonishment.

'Your cousin's father – is his accent Lebanese or Egyptian?' she is saying.

Édouard Safi sits beside Ruby. He is one of the protagonists of this story, the groom's cousin, but most importantly, the best man at this wedding. Édouard does not respond to his wife's question. Concentrating on his plate, he painstakingly removes the alfalfa sprouts, or whatever they are, covering the thin slices of beef.

The origin or nature of his cousin's father's accent is not Édouard's main concern: this meat, this very red, very – what's the word? – viscous meat, was it cooked in the oven? That is what he would like to know.

Ruby persists: 'I've never understood where the people in your family come from . . .'

Édouard would like to answer 'from the Mediterranean', but it sounds vague. A car mechanic and self-employed tow-truck operator, he dislikes being pressured.

Ruby Brume's capacity to exert pressure is unrivalled.

Édouard is annoyed by Ruby's question not because he refuses to discuss the origins of his forebears. On the contrary. The problem with the question is that the one asking it is Ruby.

Tomorrow, Édouard Safi and Ruby Brume will move into their first apartment together: the charming lower half of a duplex in a suburb on Montreal's South Shore, a stone's throw from the St Lawrence, the very river whose waters can now be seen shimmering beyond the dais in the waning late-afternoon light.

Édouard, who has had enough, replies: 'Lebanese, Egyptian, it's all the same.'

2

Shafik Elias stands a few metres away from Ruby's chair. He takes the first of the ten paces that separate him from the Cleopatra table, one of the three top tables where the newly-weds' close relations and friends are seated.

It was Sue Mechanic's idea to name the tables after cardinal cities in the newly-weds' 'history', which should be understood here in the broad sense.

Who is Sue Mechanic?

Okay, but wait.

Who is Édouard Safi?

Okay, but wait, wait.

Who is Shafik Elias?

In the course of his very brief walk, currently estimated to be fifteen paces, Shafik, father of the groom, will see the film of his life projected in fast-forward.

Not to worry: he won't stumble and hit a table corner; he won't die before the evening ends. Besides, it's impossible for this Mediterranean man to fall on a table corner: Cleopatra is not the traditional rectangular shape; it's round. Sue had no choice. The three top tables, Cleopatra, Shawinigan in the middle and Addis Ababa, are round. This is scandalous. Sue is taking the compromise very badly; it's political. For a wedding planner of her calibre, it's a nightmare.

Thus, as he moves through a parallel time, the man whose words inaugurated this story will visit, or rather, revisit, the best scenes of his life. This is his favourite film, and Shafik, like most people, never tires of remixing the key episodes.

There's no denying that this day offers a unique opportunity to add a new one: 'The Son's Wedding'. Shafik is an organized man fond of collecting memories and objects, sorting them, classifying them, storing them in boxes, folders, cameras, computers, all sorts of machines. However reserved and stoic he may be, he feels a surge of emotion, the effect of the prolonged applause, and the images projected on the screen of his mind are scrambled. The Swiss contracts appear before his mother's death, the first snow in Montreal before the Six Day War, the feluccas on the Nile before the Corniche in Alexandria, his son's wedding before that of his own father.

As the guests look at him with gleeful smiles, Shafik Elias sets out to cover the dozen metres between him and Cleopatra, where the beef carpaccio awaits him. He is about to stride back across half a century.

Events move quickly, or slowly, or normally. He blinks, a second expands, and all at once he feels many things.

We are in the middle of La Toundra on 7 July 2007. He takes a step, blinks, feels the torrid heat of his native region, and in his eyes, such a pale shade of blue, the hue of Alexandria's sky joins the deep blue of the sea, as if the colour were unable to choose.

3

The time is 8.43 p.m.

The film opens with a shot of the Mediterranean, calmer than it usually is. Perhaps you can hear the off-camera voices of men in fezzes chatting on a patio, or you may notice the streetcar entering Mahatet El Raml, literally the Station of the Sand.

Shafik Elias translates in his head as he invents the scenes and soundtrack, for he distinctly remembers that at the age of three he did not yet speak Arabic, only French. He reconstructs his Alexandria childhood, the kind that the Shawam, the Syro-Lebanese Egyptians, erstwhile colonial masters, could still give to their children. Things would change with Nasser.

Who are the native Egyptians?

The Nubians? The Copts? The Arabs who migrated from Arabia in the year 600 when the Conquest began? The Ottomans who came in the time of Muhammad Ali? And even if we were to agree on the true ethnic origin of genuine, bona fide Egyptians – even if we managed to establish that these people arrived first rather than those others, and that the former, that is, these people, were, say, the Nubians – would they be the only ones entitled to claim Egypt as their country?

Is this even the right question? A real question?

Even though it is hot on the banks of the Nile, can the genuine, bona fide Egyptians be referred to as dyed in the wool?

An amusing thought, which occurs to Shafik just as he crosses paths with his daughter-in-law's mother, a genuine, bona fide Québécoise *pure laine*; a Nubian in all but name. She is sitting at the Shawinigan table. Shafik turns his thoughts back to the archaic demonym, Shawam, singular Shami, which is what the native Egyptians called people from a certain part of the Fertile Crescent. Shafik is a Shami. His father Youssef was a Shami. His father's father Elias was a Shami. His son Youssef is not a Shami.

Shafik turns his thoughts back to the history of his country, although he is well aware that at the age of three, when the film of his life begins, he is too young to understand his country, too young to understand the Fertile Crescent, too young to understand the Middle East.

Anyway, at what age *do* you understand it.

4

Shawam because Shafik Elias's forebears came from Bilad al-Sham, a province created by the caliphates that would rule over the region for centuries. It's from this province's name, Sham, that the term Shawam derives: those who hail from Sham, the inhabitants of Sham.

Shafik knows that his family, like those of many Shawam, have lived in Egypt for two generations, his ancestors having fled persecution from Christians under the Ottoman Empire.

With his blue eyes he gazes at the sea, so very calm, sees the streetcar appear and pull into the station, and, perhaps, hears the men in fezzes.

His life has just begun. The scene unfolds in Alexandria, where Shafik's family rents a spacious apartment less than a kilometre from the Corniche, in the heart of the Cleopatra district. Youssef, his father, and Marcelle, his mother, treat their only son to simple pleasures: pastry from Chez Délices, an ice cream from Fayumi's.

Shafik can still remember the names of these shops. Uttering them in his mind fifty-five years later unleashes sensations and images that have been buried in his memory. He holds a small wooden knick-knack brought back from Switzerland by a friend of his father's, sees it in his hand, recalls the fragrance of jasmine, powerful and undiminished, perfuming the street where he was born; hears his mother singing an Umm Kulthum song while she prepares his sports bag and ties his shoelaces, as she sits in the living-room sun.

The child is too sheltered to be aware of what is happening in July 1952. The Mediterranean grows rough as *El Mahrousa*, the yacht of newly deposed King Farouk, reaches the Côte d'Azur.

He takes another step, moves away from the dais, crosses the threshold of a memory, plunges into that dark October; he has just turned six.

For months now his parents have been telling him excitedly that he will soon have a little sister, a little brother, and that for his father and mother this will be a true miracle.

Doctors who have recently returned to Alexandria with European degrees are using a new procedure, which makes it possible to treat the uterine problem that has prevented his mother's pregnancies from going to full term.

His parents have almost lost count of the miscarriages: two before he was born, three since – they aren't sure any more.

His mother is unable to stay pregnant.

Shafik realizes that if he can be in this world, and if he can walk towards his table of honour in the twenty-first century, it is because in the Egypt of his childhood, when men wore fezzes and pastries could be enjoyed on the Corniche, his mother was bedridden for a full seven months; it is because his mother, *ya umi ya khalwa*, stopped living her life for seven months, *allah yar hamak*.

What exactly is her medical problem?

Shafik Elias remembers a single instruction – 'raise the uterus' – which he so often heard following the tragedy. Still today, he has no idea what this might mean; he has never asked an obstetrician, even when his wife was pregnant with his son.

How can one explain that the desire for a second child could lead a young woman to her grave? From the conjugal bed to the final resting place? How can he accept that his mother did not keep her promise to come back the day after the procedure?

Too many questions.

This Mediterranean man no longer sees things from his own point of view; above, he sees a very dark living room, curtained windows. A few black-clad great-aunts gather around him. They impart to him the saddest, most momentous news of his life: your *maman* has died, *ya* Shafik, your *maman* has gone up to heaven. From now on the Virgin Mary will be your *maman*.

Ya umi ya khalwa, allah yar hamak.

My mother, my beautiful mother. May God keep your soul.

5

Shafik has abdominal pains. Ever since he was young, the inflammation has gnawed away at the walls of his intestines, just as it gnaws away at the walls of his son's. Still, he advances resolutely, takes another step towards Cleopatra, and then he blinks: he is holding his father's hand the spring after his mother died. The little boy is among the guests at a wedding.

Shafik is wearing a silk shirt and a small white tailor-made suit; he hates the touch of silk on his skin, a sensation he remembers even now, and he has never worn silk since. The wedding Shafik is attending is not his son's but rather his father's, a marriage described as hasty, but never to his father's face.

Moving forward in La Toundra, Shafik finds it impossible to clearly analyze what must have taken place – it's distant, painful and, most of all, futile. He calls her *maman*, the woman his father is

marrying six months after Marcelle's death; he called her *maman* –
she was his mother.

The tension in Egypt has come to a head. The new Nasser regime
is sliding towards the brink in its relations with the European forces
still stationed in Egypt. The breach is imminent.

In a few months' time, the first of three wars that this Mediterranean
man was to live through breaks out, three wars that will place the
Shawam in the double bind of being too European in the eyes of
old-stock Egyptians to truly denounce the colonial forces, and too
Egyptian to have – like the colonists – a country where they might
find refuge, where they could return before the flare-up.

Shafik can still hear his father in the kitchen one fateful July
night, telling his second wife: 'Our origins deprive us of the right
to be patriots.' Yet the Mediterranean man can also remember his
father's pride when, on 26 July 1956, four years to the day after
King Farouk's abdication, Nasser takes control of the Suez Canal
and sets in motion the process that would lead to its nationalization
and the sequestering of assets that had belonged to the European
industrialists since the nineteenth century. But his father's pride turns
into disquiet as everyone grows more mindful of the looming danger.

Even though he is not yet seven, even though the Suez Expedition,
as it is sometimes called, lasts only nine days, Shafik can recall every
detail, every event, every moment of fear and anxiety of that first
war: the blue drapes his father hangs over the windows to make them
invisible to the fighter planes, the song all the neighbours sing as they
too put up drapes, the sandbags in front of the entranceways to the
house, the underground shelters where people go to shield themselves
from shrapnel, the noise and blaze of the Egyptian anti-aircraft
defence deploying parabolas of light in the sky over Alexandria.

The war breaks out at the end of October; France, the United
Kingdom and Israel launch Operation Musketeer. The objective is
to overthrow Nasser and take back the canal. The Egyptian army
is roundly beaten; the European powers order Nasser to return the
canal, but the Ra'īs refuses. The response: a wave of bombardments

by French and British warplanes to bring Nasser to his knees.

The world had changed. Despite their victory, the UK and France – caught between their American ally, then in the process of consolidating its power in the region, and the nuclear threats made by Nasser's new ally, the Soviets – are obliged to accept a ceasefire.

Shafik Elias takes another step towards Cleopatra, sees Yolande Safi, his ex-wife, his son's mother. Talking up a storm, she reigns brazenly over Addis Ababa. All eyes are on her. Around the table, the members of her family, of course: her brother Nabil in a wheelchair, her aunt from Pierrefonds, and two cousins who have come from Beirut for the occasion, but also some nosy neighbours from Little Lebanon. Shafik must admit – and so must you – that Yolande cuts a fine figure in her imperial crêpe dress.

How did things come to this?

Fifteen years of internecine warfare, three trials, a hundred thousand dollars in lawyers' fees . . .

How is it they never managed to find common ground, to make room for diplomacy, whereas the greatest conflicts of his life always managed to resolve themselves?

Shafik recalls this fact: the first deployment of Blue Berets in Egypt was organized by a Canadian, Lester B. Pearson, and this diplomatic solution to the crisis handed Nasser's regime, despite a humiliating military defeat, a political victory with dire repercussions for many Egyptians of immigrant stock.

6

The memory of the repercussions is sharper in Shafik Elias's mind than those of the war itself because his family is plagued by the nightmare of history. Scarcely a year after his mother's death, it's to the Mediterranean Sea that seven-year-old Shafik must bid adieu when his father is forced to transplant his family from Alexandria to Cairo.

Why this move with a sick child, a barely consummated second marriage, a year of upheavals from which recovery will be difficult? You raise good questions. Think work, think necessity: for all these years, Shafik's father, Youssef, has been working for a Swiss pharmaceutical company with subsidiaries in numerous countries, including Egypt. The Egyptian branch belongs to French nationals living in Cairo. Now the war, the 1956 Suez Expedition, has rendered the government openly hostile towards anyone from France, the UK or Israel. The English and the French are the first to be affected. Later on, it would be the turn of the Shawam.

When the Egyptian government seizes the company where his father is employed and expels the owners from the country, Shafik naturally has to move to Cairo. Shafik's father will coordinate the delicate transfer of the company to the government-appointed sequestrate.

Youssef and his new wife leave Alexandria with their hearts in their boots.

At 8.44 p.m., a young woman, all smiles, pops up in front of Shafik Elias as he makes his way towards Cleopatra.

It's Myriam, the maid of honour. You should see her face, her smile, her face on this day; even now, as I write this, the memory remains indelible: a slice of the sun. When this scene unfolds, she has just celebrated her twenty-eighth spring. Virginie Lavrovsky, the bride, considers her a sister. She is loved and included in the family. This is Myriam, this is Mym, Virginie's oldest friend. They met in the mid-eighties, in a schoolyard in the Notre-Dame-de-Grâce district. Something had happened that morning, a rare occurrence in the life of a child. A bird had died. They had buried it. And today, on the morning of the wedding, in the windy heat, these two lifetime friends, the bride and the maid of honour, they have every reason to hark back to that event, though you will never know why.

Here, at 8.44 p.m., Shafik Elias, on seeing Myriam, a modern young woman, a Levantine beauty, hold her arms out to him, Shafik Elias, over there, is moved at the thought that his son and daughter-in-law's best friend is a woman whose background is not so far removed from his own, for Myriam's family, over the three decades preceding their respective exiles, had endured the same perils, the same anguish, the same wars as Shafik's family.

In fact, when asked to approve the guest list, Shafik had insisted that Myriam's father, who had been one of the Israel Defense Forces paratroopers deployed in the Sinai, be invited. Shafik's son, a chronic blunderer, told Sue to seat him at the Jerusalem table, prompting Shafik to shake his head and sigh.

Myriam steps up to Shafik and kisses him on the cheek.

'I loved what you said about the sacrament of marriage. Your father married twice, just like you? And is it true that your family name means "marriage" in Arabic? That's totally insane!'

'Yes, my beautiful Mimi, "joy" or "marriage", although they're not always synonymous!'

Before they part, Shafik kisses Myriam on the cheek, that is, he kisses her, in the mandatory Lebanese manner, three times. For the wedding, Myriam has chosen a saffron-coloured illusion tulle dress. Shafik watches her move away, his heart swelling at the sight of Virginie, all smiles in her white lace. Shafik hopes that the moment will last, that love will last, that friendship will last, that life will last, and that Youssef will not see the joys of matrimony superseded by a separation and a second marriage.

Two times is a repetition. Three times is a tradition, or a curse.

Shafik hopes things will be simpler for his son, that life will be easy, but he knows that for Youssef things are complicated. Forever restless, he has a problem with the order of things, their surface, their reverse side, their content. Would you like an example? That dress in which Myriam is walking away, bathed in the fire of the waning daylight. Shafik's son will hold it in his hands for a long time and will see emanating from the illusion tulle the bygone lights of the evening that you are witnessing.

7

S hafik takes a step, resumes his forward progress, the images recommence: he sees himself as a boy again, moving in with his family near Midan Ramses, in Cairo, opposite the train station, which is dominated by a huge statue of the pharaoh Ramses II. He sees himself in the corridors of St Jean-Baptiste de La Salle, the Cairo institution of the Frères des Écoles chrétiennes, on his first day of school.

He skims over the difficult years of his childhood, years marked by rheumatism, the first doses of cortisone, the terrible abdominal pains that would go undiagnosed for so long, pains for which the intravenous immunomodulator treatment that his son receives now had not yet been developed. Like father, like son. The disease. Sometimes twice can also be a curse.

Shafik skips over a decade of childhood suffering and ends up face-to-face with himself, at eighteen, on the threshold of an uncertain future. Like most Shawam, he is educated, speaks the right languages, knows the right people. He goes to high-society soirées in the wealthy suburb of Heliopolis, celebrations at the Institut Français d'Egypte au Caire, garden parties in the grounds of foreign embassies in Zamalek.

He opens himself up to the outside world; during his summers back in Alexandria he courts young European women and enjoys the charms of the San Stefano beach.

He has his first adult experiences, through which he discovers another Cairo, another Alexandria; the cities that he thought were so intimately familiar to him expand and are coupled with parallel cities, private itineraries, where the interesting spots are suddenly no longer Pharos Island or the Giza pyramids, but a certain bachelor apartment, a certain inner courtyard at a certain friend's house, a certain bar in the shining night. If memory serves, it's during that period that his father first takes him to one of Umm Kulthum's monthly concerts. Shafik and his father feel a strong attachment to the singer, who is a model of resilience, and nothing is more admired in this family than resilience.

Don't complain, *ya* Shafik, you have the sea and the sky, and life is better if you don't deny suffering.

Yowm 'asal, yowm basal. A day of honey follows a day of onions.

8

It's a June morning like any other. A morning when, before the sirens begin to sound, Shafik's worries are mundane: passing his exams at the School of Engineering. These are short-term worries, the kind that don't trigger panic attacks.

Relations between those old foes, Egypt and Israel, are strained to the utmost, and soon there will be gunfire rippling along the banks of the Nile.

The invigilators shout that everyone must leave the campus and return home. With his friends and a dozen students he doesn't know, Shafik crosses the Zakher Bridge. They realize that bridges are the first strategic targets, and an as yet contained terror runs through them like a silent shock wave. They enter the suspended time of war. The university will be shut down for weeks. Shafik remembers the dilated moments and the impact of events happening so swiftly that everything is already too late, irremediable, ruined. The war would last all of six days, but the consequences are still apparent half a century on, as his son gets married, as you read this story in the pages of *Granta* in 2017, or maybe many years later.

But if Shafik remembers the war so clearly, it's also because it marked a turning point in the relationship between the Shawam and their native Egypt.

Shafik recalls the atmosphere prevailing in Cairo on the night of the first bombardments, the frenzy of the Cairenes streaming into the streets for a victory celebration after absorbing every drop of propaganda produced by the state-run radio station.

Each day, his father listens to the foreign radio stations: Radio Monte Carlo, Voice of America, Radio Beirut, Kol Israel, the BBC, all of them broadcasting via shortwave.

These stations paint a catastrophic picture of Egypt's military situation: half its aviation destroyed in a few hours, the country fallen without resistance, the Israelis expanding their territory threefold in less than a week.

Shafik still feels the sting of humiliation. As he nears his table, embraces his second wife, who has just left Cleopatra to join him, while taking care – you guessed it – to be seen by Yolande, Shafik tries to put out of his mind the fatalistic potentiality of politics, of which war – as a great military theorist once said – is the continuation by other means; in the Middle East, throughout Shafik's youth, this could be put more simply: war is the continuation of war.

As he slowly makes his way towards Cleopatra and sees the waiters taking away dishes that have hardly been touched, he exchanges a coupon for a chicken from the shelves of a state cooperative, and brings it back to his father, who can now cheerfully prepare the Sunday-afternoon feast, the ceremonial *mulukhiya*, the green soup: a whole chicken cut into pieces, rice, a blend of broth and *mulukhiya* – the main component of this meal, a plant known in English as Jew's mallow – pickled onions, toasted bread.

9

On a Saturday afternoon in October 1973, leaving his laboratory in Cairo, Shafik accompanies an old schoolmate to the Canadian embassy, near Midan Tahrir, where he must pick up a residence permit.

His old schoolmate's appointment drags on, and Shafik gets out his transistor radio, tunes in the Sawt al-Arab station. It must be around 2.15 p.m. when the news breaks: Egyptian troops, under the command of Sadat and Mubarak, had set out to reconquer the Sinai and after a few hours succeeded in crossing first the canal and then the Bar-Lev Line. Shafik does not wait for the historians, from whom he would later learn that the Egyptians' surprise attack was launched in the middle of the Yom Kippur fasting period. He turns off the radio. There is no one in line at the embassy's reception desk and he makes the most important decision of his life. This is the last war he will live through in Egypt. He stands up, takes a step, then one more, and greets the woman behind the desk in his best French. One thing leads to another, from this initial discussion until his visa, he doesn't quite understand how it came about, but here he is seated in a Boeing 747. Shafik emigrates to Canada.

When he arrives at Cleopatra, just before sitting down to eat his carpaccio, he scans the room, and, to his surprise, he does not see his son anywhere in La Toundra.

The bridegroom isn't there.

For an instant, Shafik is filled with apprehension, the fear that preys on every parent. He is afraid *something* has happened. He looks in the direction of Addis Ababa, nods to Yolande, who appears untroubled. All their lives, they would fret about their son in different ways: she is nervous of draughts, excessive perspiration, the mixing of different foods; he, anxious about his son's path in the world, his performance in school, his ability to find a good job. Both of them wrong, both of them right.

Shafik is bewildered. He imagined his son would be waiting for him in front of Cleopatra, amid the applause, to thank him for his speech, his words, his presence.

As he is about to sit down at last, he remembers taking leave of his own father at Cairo airport thirty years earlier. Then he thinks back to his arrival in Montreal, to the surge of anxiety as he alights from the airplane because he has just sixty dollars in his pocket. Very soon, he would find employment, exhausting, mind-deadening work. In his capacity as a chemical engineer, he inspects containers unloaded in the port. The conditions are brutal and, with ships docking twenty-four hours a day, he must often work at night. Two weeks on, he loses his footing in a sugar container and cracks his skull. The blood flows down over his eyes. He is twenty-six years old. And days of onions follow days of honey.

A month later, in the cold and damp of November, he receives a telegram from a friend: YOUR FATHER PASSED AWAY IN ALEXANDRIA ARRANGEMENTS MADE NO NEED TO COME MOTHER OK LETTER WILL FOLLOW.

Shafik casts his eyes towards the end of the room, looking for Youssef, but the images accelerate, pulling him backwards. He sees his son, nestled, newborn, in the arms of Yolande at the Royal Victoria Hospital. It's one o'clock in the morning. Time folds in on itself; everything returns: the red and green wallpaper on the ground floor of their new house in Cartierville, the mornings when Youssef, standing on the toilet, watches him shave, the summers building sandcastles on the beaches of New Jersey, meeting Yolande in Little Italy, Youssef and Édouard stepping out of a jail cell with no laces on their shoes, little Youssef as John the Apostle in a play at Catholic primary school, and now, as through your eyes, Shafik finally sits down at Cleopatra, at his son's wedding. He sees himself seeing himself, overwhelmed by the whirling images. He unbuttons his jacket, settles into his chair and lifts his head. The blue of his shining eyes is unreal.

Shafik looks over at Shawinigan, but Youssef is not there. Virginie is radiant and gives him a wide, knowing grin. The room is abuzz with laughter and conversation.

Night is falling, it's 8.48 p.m., and Shafik Elias Farah finally turns his head in my direction, at the far end of La Toundra, near the Jardin des Floralies, at precisely the moment when, zipping up my fly, I step out through the plate-glass door. ■

Nouveau Projet

The best new writing and ideas from Québec, twice a year.

Canadian Magazine of the Year, 2015
Canadian Magazine of the Year finalist, 2014, 2016 and 2017

nouveauprojet.com

Souvankham Thammavongsa with her parents, Sisouvanh and Phouk, and her brother, John, after their Canadian citizenship ceremony, Ottawa, 1983
Courtesy of the author

HOW TO PRONOUNCE KNIFE

Souvankham Thammavongsa

The note had been typed out, folded over two times. It had been pinned to the child's chest. It could not be missed. And like all the other notes that went home with the child, her mother removed the pin and threw it away. If the contents were important, a phone call would be made to the home. And there had been no such call.

The family lived in a small apartment with two rooms. On the wall of the main room was a tiny painting with a brown bend at the centre. That brown bend was supposed to be a bridge, and the blots of red and orange brushed in around it were supposed to be trees. It was her father who had painted this. Now he doesn't paint anything like that, not since he started at the print shop, smelling like the paint thinner he was around all day. That smell, like lady nail polish, never left him, not even after he'd had a shower. When he came home, first thing he always did was kick off his shoes. Then, he'd hand over a roll of newspaper to the child, who unfolded sheets on the floor, forming a square, and around that square they sat down to have dinner.

For dinner, it was cabbage and chitterlings. The butcher either threw the stuff away or had it out on display for cheap so her mother bought bags and bags from him and put them in the fridge. There were so many ways to cook these: in a broth with ginger and noodles, grilled over charcoal fire, stewed with the bits that came from the discards, or the way the child liked them best – baked in the oven with lemongrass and salt. When the child took these items to school, other children would tease her about the smell. What that smell was that was so bad, the child had no idea. 'You all don't know what a delicacy is. You wouldn't know a good thing even if it came five hundred pounds and sat on your face! Fools, you are.'

When they all sat down for dinner, the child thought of the note, about bringing it to her father. There had been so many, but maybe this one was important. Her father thought about his pay and his friends and how they were all making their living now. He himself wasn't educated, but the ones who were found themselves picking worms or being managed by pimple-faced teenagers. When the child got up and brought the note over to him, her father waved it away, said, 'Later.' He said this in Lao. And then he remembered. He said, in Lao, 'Don't speak Lao and don't tell anyone you are Lao. It's no good to tell people where you're from.' The child looked to the centre of her father's chest, where, on this T-shirt, four letters stood side by side: LAOS.

A few weeks after that, there was some commotion in the class. All the girls showed up wearing different variations of pink and the boys had on dark suits and little knotted ties. Miss Choi, the grade 1 teacher, was wearing a purple dress, dotted with a print of tiny white flowers, and shoes with little heels. The child looked down at what she was wearing. She was out of place in her green jogging suit which had been bought at Honest Ed's, that place with all the flashing lights where they lined up to get a free turkey for Christmas. The green was dark, like the green of broccoli, and the fabric at the knees was a few shades lighter and it took their shape even when she was standing straight up. In this scene of pink and sparkles and matching purses and black bow ties and pressed collars, she saw she was not like the others.

Miss Choi noticed the green the child was wearing and her eyes widened. They calmly blinked, always scanning the room for something out of place, and when she spotted something she didn't like her eyes got like this. All big and alarmed. She came running over and said, 'Joy.

Did you get your parents to read the note we sent home with you?'

'No,' she lied, looking at the floor where her blue shoes fitted themselves inside the space of the square of a small tile. Now, she didn't want to lie, but there was no point in embarrassing her parents. The day went as planned. And in the class photo, the child was seated a little off to the side, with the grade and year sign placed in front of her. The sign was always right in the middle of these photos, but the photographer had to do something to hide the dirt of her shoes. Above that sign, she smiled.

When her mother came to get her after school she asked why it was all the others were dressed up this way, but the child didn't tell her. The child lied, saying, to her mother, 'I don't know. All of them are out of their minds, thinking they could be fancy on an ordinary day. An ordinary day! It's all it is. Don't you pay your mind to them. Not one second!'

The child came home with a book. It was for practice, to read on her own. The book the child was given had pictures and a few words. The picture was supposed to explain a little bit about what was going on with the words, but there was this one word that didn't have a picture. It was there by itself, and when she pronounced each letter, the word didn't sound like anything real. She didn't know how to pronounce it.

After dinner, the three of them sat down together on the bare floor, watching television side by side. From behind, the child looked like her father. Her hair had been cut short in the shape of a bowl. The child's shoulders drooped and her spine bent like there was some weight she was carrying there, like she knew what a day of hard work was all about. Before long the television pictures changed into vertical stripes the colour of a rainbow, and her parents stumbled into bed. Most nights, the child followed, but tonight she was bothered by what she didn't know and wanted to know it. She opened the book and went looking for that word. The one that didn't sound like anything she knew.

That one.

It was her last chance before her father would go off to bed. He was the only one in their home who knew how to read. She brought the book to him and pointed to the word, asked what it was. He leaned over it and said, 'Kah-nnn-eye-ffff. It's kahneyff.' That's what it sounded like to him, what it was.

It was the next day that all of this was to come out. What this word was. Miss Choi gathered the whole class together. They all sat around the green carpet at the front of the room while the desks were left empty, and she would get someone to read. Someone would volunteer or she would point at someone, and on this day Miss Choi looked around and found the child. 'You, Joy, you haven't read yet. Why don't you get your book and read for us.'

The child started and went along just fine until she got to that word. The one that didn't sound like anything she knew. Miss Choi pointed to it and then tapped at the page as if by doing so the sound would spill itself forth. But the child didn't know and there was no one to ask. Tap. Tap. Tap. Finally, a girl in the class called out, 'It is knife! The "k" is silent,' and rolled her eyes as if there was nothing easier in the world to know.

This yellow-haired girl had blue eyes and freckles dotted around her nose. This girl's mother was always seen after school honking in the parking lot in a big shiny black car with a 'v' and a 'w' holding each other inside a circle. Her mother owned for herself a black fur coat and walked in heels like it was Picture Day every day. And sometimes it would be her father there. He was no different. Always honking on about something too. This girl read loud and clear. She never stopped to account for the spaces between the words. It was like something she knew by heart. And every time this girl volunteered to read, what she read came out perfect. They all tried and many had come so close. One or two errors could mean not seeing Miss Choi's red velvet sack with all the prizes in it. For this girl, the sack always appeared. On this very day the prize was a red yo-yo. A red yo-yo! It was grand. There had been others before: a pencil, a pack of chewing gum, a lollipop, even a sack of marbles. But none had been as lovely as this red yo-yo.

And had the child known what that word was, that red yo-yo would have been hers, but, of course, all of it would remain locked in the top drawer of Miss Choi's desk now.

When the school day was over, the child gathered up her things. All that she had fit into a white plastic grocery bag. Now, for some reason, Miss Choi was waiting for her near the door and when she got there she asked the child to follow her to the front desk. There, she unlocked the top drawer and pulled out the red velvet sack. 'Pick one,' she said. And the child reached inside and pulled out a paper thing. It was a puzzle with an airplane in the sky.

Later that night, the child does not tell her father the 'k' in knife is silent. She doesn't tell him about being in the principal's office, about being told of rules and how things are the way they are. It was just a letter, she was told, but that single letter, out there alone, and in the front, was why she was in the office in the first place. She doesn't tell how she had insisted the letter 'k' was not silent. It couldn't be and she had argued and argued, 'It's in the front! The first one! It should have a sound. Why isn't there a sound there?' and then, she screamed as if they had taken some important thing away. She never gave up on what her father said, on that first sound there. And none of them, with all their lifetimes of reading and good education, could explain it.

And later, at home, the child looked over at her father. How he picked up each grain of rice with his chopsticks, not dropping a single one. How he ate, clearing everything in his bowl. How small and shrunken he seemed. She thought of what else he didn't know. What else she would have to find out for herself. She wanted to tell her father that some letters, even though they are there, we do not say them. But decided, now was not the time to say such a thing. Now, the child said nothing. She told her father only that she won something, this thing, and showed him the prize. He did not know what it was she could have won. He is delighted because, in some way, he has won it too. They take the prize, all the little pieces of it, and start forming the edge, the blue sky, the other pieces, the middle. The whole picture, they fill those in later. ∎

Gary Barwin

Essay

in this essay, you will explore the proposition that:

the heart is an ocean-sized drum
a rat-sized jellyfish
a capsized ballcap
a sheep the size of night

also that:

the current century is transparent and
we can see clear to the other side

when I woke and began writing this question for you
I felt as if each of my eyes were a thousand miles apart
and I was shiny

and you in front of a bowl of soup
my heart in the spoon in your hand

what would our world have been if soup were impossible
in your answer, make reference to:

the force of gravity, the three states of matter
the small bones of a lover's foot

was I:

a.   shiny as a spoon
b.   shiny as a bus-station locker filled with Greek gods—
      parallel translucent honey-coloured rays from the door vent
      beaming across the bus station which those waiting
      mistake for nostalgia, a stroke,
      the honey-coloured radiant and kind essence of the world,
      finally revealed
c.   actually a form of shinny

The first paragraph of the body should contain the strongest argument, most significant example, cleverest illustration, or an obvious beginning point. The heart beats as if an ocean-sized drum, each rat-sized jellyfish lifted then dropped by the waves which move to its rhythm. I am frozen. My thoughts heaped like night on the back of gorse flowers. Never suggest that you don't know what you're talking about or that you're not enough of an expert that your opinion would matter. You and I are transparent and would have been impossible except for spoons. We lift the broth and drink. We are a thousand miles away. A final statement gives the reader signals that the discussion has come to an end. I imagine the small bones of your feet, invisible constellations reconfigured with each step.

Final mark: /30.

BLANKET TOSS UNDER MIDNIGHT SUN

Paul Seesequasis

Three years ago my mother, a residential school survivor, told me she was 'tired of hearing just negative things about those times'; that there had been 'positive and strong things in Indigenous communities then'. Inspired by her words, I began to look through archives, libraries, museums and private collections in search of images of Indigenous life that reflected integrity, strength, resourcefulness, hard work, family and play. And I found them.

The following photographs are of Indigenous peoples in primarily what is now Canada taken, for the most part, by non-Indigenous photographers between 1925 and the 1970s. When I first began to post some of these archival photographs on Twitter and Facebook, I expected some people to follow and 'like' them, but I could never have predicted that people would write in saying, 'That's my grandmother!' or 'That's me forty-two years ago!', often having seen the photograph for the very first time. This brought another layer to the photographs: the act of naming, a form of reclamation.

History has, since I was a child, interested me, but I am neither a trained historian nor an archivist, so I entered into this wet behind the ears, learning as I went along. I stumbled, made assumptions occasionally that were in error, and was grateful when I was corrected. I also learned that archival notes were not always accurate, either in name, location or cultural identity. There were lessons to be repeated like a mantra. Never assume. Worse, never add your assumptions to the captions. Reprint the archival captions as they are but expect, in many cases, that they will be inaccurate. Hope that in the seeing, someone out there will recognise a face, a hill, a building. Finally, expect the unexpected. ■

Children (Dene), Délı̨ne, Northwest Territories, 1968
© HENRY BUSSE / NORTHWEST TERRITORIES ARCHIVES

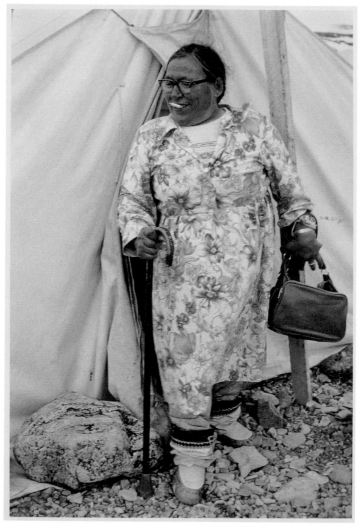

Martha Angugattiaq Ungaalaaq (Inuk), Steensby Inlet, Nunavut, 1975
© ROBERT SEMENIUK / LIBRARY AND ARCHIVES CANADA

Annie Johannesee, Johnny and unnamed person, Kuujjuaq, Nunavik, *c*.1960
© ROSEMARY GILLIAT EATON/LIBRARY AND ARCHIVES CANADA

Rosemary Gilliat Eaton, self-portrait, Gatineau, Quebec, *c.*1962
© ROSEMARY GILLIAT EATON / LIBRARY AND ARCHIVES CANADA

Emma Alfred with beaver purse (Kwanlin Dün), Pelly River, Yukon, *c.*1966
© CATHARINE MCCLELLAN / CANADIAN MUSEUM OF HISTORY

Charles Bobbish, Gordon Neacappo, Stephen Lameboy and John Pashagumeskum (Cree), Fort George, Quebec, 1973
© GEORGE LEGRADY

James Jerome, self-portrait (Gwich'in), Inuvik, Northwest Territories, *c.*1977
© HENRY BUSSE/NORTHWEST TERRITORIES ARCHIVES

Boy with red cap (Inuk), Nunavut or Nunavik, *c.*1960
© ROSEMARY GILLIAT EATON / LIBRARY AND ARCHIVES CANADA

Bessie Martin (Dene), Dettah, Northwest Territories, 1970
© HENRY BUSSE / NORTHWEST TERRITORIES ARCHIVES

Seal hunt (Inuit), Frobisher Bay, 1960
© ROSEMARY GILLIAT EATON/LIBRARY AND ARCHIVES CANADA

Hunting trip (Cree), Eastmain, Quebec, 1973
© GEORGE LEGRADY

George Johnston's Taxi Service: Angela Tom, unnamed person and Fanny Tom (Tlingit), Teslin, Yukon, 1944
© GEORGE JOHNSTON COLLECTION/YUKON ARCHIVES – DEPARTMENT OF TOURISM AND CULTURE

Visiting Eastmain (Cree), Eastmain, Quebec, 1973
© GEORGE LEGRADY

Man in bow of freight canoe (Cree), Eastmain, Quebec, 1973
© GEORGE LEGRADY

Sheouak Petaulassie, son and unnamed person (Inuit), Cape Dorset, Nunavut, 1960
© ROSEMARY GILLIAT EATON / LIBRARY AND ARCHIVES CANADA

Dora Grandejambe with dog (Dene), Fort Good Hope, Northwest Territories, 1969
© HENRY BUSSE/NORTHWEST TERRITORIES ARCHIVES

Kids outside tipi (Cree, Saulteaux, Dakota, Assiniboine), Qu'Appelle Valley, Saskatchewan, 1957

Cars at powwow (Dakota), Qu'Appelle Valley, Saskatchewan, 1957
© EVERETT BAKER / SASKATCHEWAN HISTORY & FOLKLORE SOCIETY

At Ghost River (Blackfoot), Ghost River, Alberta, 1962
© ROSEMARY GILLIAT EATON / LIBRARY AND ARCHIVES CANADA

THE BLUE CLERK

Dionne Brand

Verso 1 *The back of a leaf*

What is said and what is unsaid; what is written and what is withheld. What is withheld is on the left-hand page. These are left-hand pages. The moment they are written they will not exist. That is, they will not exist as themselves. As they were first conceived. What is withheld is on the back of the leaf.

I have withheld more than I have written. I have restrained more than I have given. I have left unsaid more than I have said. I have withheld much more than I have withheld. Even these nine left-handed pages have already created their own left-handed pages, as will be seen. I will have added for clarification or withdrawn some detail. I will have parsed the structure of the sentence and the meaning of the sentence and reformulated it to resolve some understanding that was tentative in the first place but that merely for the sake of agreeing to a rule of syntax I have to present as certain. Moreover, I will have cleaned out all of my doubt, or all of my prevarication, or all of my timidity.

The left-hand page is a recursive page; each verso becomes a recto. Each left-handed page generates one right-handed page and an infinite number of left-handed pages.

What is withheld multiplies. The left-handed pages accumulate with more speed and intensity than the right-handed pages.

They are chronic. That is to say, they are always present, occurring, intrinsic and incurable, unfailing and uneasy like freight. The freight of withholding, gathered over years, becomes heavier and heavier. Indefinite and unbounded weight.

Verso 1.1

There are bales of paper on a wharf somewhere, at a port, somewhere. There is a clerk inspecting and inspecting them. She is the blue clerk. She is dressed in a blue ink coat, her right hand is dry, her left hand is dripping; she is expecting a ship, she is preparing for one. Though she is afraid that by the time the ship arrives the stowage will have overtaken the wharf.

The sea off the port is roiling some days, calm some days.

Up and down the wharf she examines the bales, shifts old left-handed pages to the back, making room for the swift voluminous incoming freight.

The clerk looks out sometimes over the roiling sea or over the calm sea, finding the horizon, seeking the transfiguration of the ship.

The bales have been piling up for years yet they look brightly scored, crisp and sharp. They have abilities the clerk is forever curtailing and marshalling. They are stacked deep and high and the clerk, in her inky garment, weaves in and out of them checking and rechecking that they do not find their way into the right-hand page. She scrutinises the manifest hourly, the contents and sequence of loading. She keeps account of cubic metres of senses, perceptions and resistant facts. No one need be aware of these, no one is likely to understand, some of these are quite dangerous and some of them are too delicate and beautiful for the present world.

There are green unclassified aphids for example living with these papers.

The sky over the wharf is a sometimish sky, it changes with the moods and anxieties of the clerk, it is ink blue as her coat or grey as the sea or pink as the evening clouds.

The sun is like a red wasp that flies in and out of the clerk's ear. It escapes the clerk's flapping arms.

The clerk would like a cool moon but all the weather depends on the left-handed pages. All the acridity in the salt air, all the waft of almonds and seaweed, all the sharp poisonous odour of time.

The left-handed pages swell like dunes some years. It is all the clerk can do to mount them with her theodolite, to survey their divergent lines of intention. These dunes would envelop her as well as the world if she were not the ink-drenched clerk.

Some years the aridity of the left-hand pages makes the air dusty, parches the hand of the clerk. The dock is then a desert, the bales turned to sand and the clerk must arrange each grain in the correct order, humidify them with her breath and wait for the season to pass.

And some years the pages absorb all the water in the air becoming like four-hundred-year-old wood and the dock weeps and creaks and the clerk's garment sweeps sodden through the bales and the clerk weeps and wonders why she is here and when will the ship ever arrive.

I am the clerk, overwhelmed by the left-handed page. Each blooming quire contains a thought selected out of many reams of thoughts and vetted by the clerk, then presented to the author. The clerk replaces the file, which has grown to a size, unimaginable.

I am the author in charge of the ink-stained clerk pacing the dock. I record the right-hand page. I do nothing really because what I do is clean. I forget the bales of paper fastened to the dock and the weather doesn't bother me. I choose the presentable things, the beautiful things. And I enjoy them sometimes, if not for the clerk.

The clerk has the worry and the damp thoughts, and the arid thoughts.

Now where will I put that new folio. There's no room where it came from, it's withheld so much this time, so much about . . . this and that . . . never mind; that will only make it worse.

The clerk goes balancing the newly withheld pages across the ink-slippery dock. She throws an eye on the still sea; the weather is concrete today, her garment is stiff like marl today.

Verso 1.1.01

When Borges says he remembers his father's library in Buenos Aires, the gaslight, the shelves and the voice of his father reciting Keats' 'Ode to a Nightingale', I recall the library at the roundabout on Harris Promenade. The library near the Metro Cinema and the Woolworths store. But to go back, first when my eyes lit on Borges' dissertation, I thought, 'I had no library.' And I thought it with my usual melancholy and next my usual pride in being without.

And the first image that came to me after that was my grandfather's face with his tortoiseshell spectacles and his weeping left eye and his white shirt and his dark seamed trousers and his newspaper and his moustache and his clips around his shirt arms and his notebooks and his logbooks; and at the same moment that the melancholy came it was quickly brushed aside by the thought that he was my library.

In his notebooks, my grandfather logged hundredweight of copra, pounds of chick feed and manure; the health of horses, the nails for their iron shoes; the acreages of coconut and tania; the nuisance of heliconia; the depth of two rivers; the length of a rainy season.

Then I returned to the Harris Promenade and the white library with wide steps, but when I ask, there was no white library with wide steps, they tell me, but an ochre library at a corner with great steps leading up. What made me think it was a white library? The St Paul's Anglican Church anchoring the lime-white Promenade, the colonial white courthouse, the grey-white public hospital overlooking the sea? I borrowed a book at that white library even though the library as I imagine it now did not exist. A book by Gerald Durrell, namely, *My Family and Other Animals*. I don't remember any other books I brought home, though I remember a feeling of quiet luxury and a desire for spectacles to seem as intelligent as my grandfather. And I read too in this white library a scrap about Don Quixote and Sancho Panza, though only the kind of scrap, the kind of refuse, or onion skin, they give schoolchildren in colonial countries about a strange skinny man on a horse with a round sidekick.

The ochre library on Harris Promenade was at the spot that was called 'library corner' and it used to be very difficult to get to because of the traffic and the narrow sidewalk. But I was agile and small. And I thought I was ascending a wide white-stepped library. And though that was long ago, I remember the square clock adjacent to the roundabout. And I can see the Indian cinema next door, papered with the film *Aarti* starring Meena Kumari and Ashok Kumar.

My grandfather with his logs and notebooks lived in a town by the sea. That sea was like a lucent page to the left of the office where my grandfather kept his logs and notebooks with their accounts. Apart from the depth of the two rivers, namely the Iguana and the Pilot, he also noted the tides and the times of their rising and falling.

ßmoon rise	5.34 a.m.	
high tide	5.48 a.m.	0.82 ft
sunrise	5.56 a.m.	
low tide	12.40 p.m.	0.03 ft
new moon	4.45 p.m.	
sunset	6.23 p.m.	
high tide	6.33 p.m.	0.56 ft
low tide	12.02 a.m.	0.16 ft

Spring tides, the greatest change between high and low, neap tides, the least.

And, the rain, the number of inches and its absence. He needed to know about the rain for sunning and drying the copra. And, too, he kept a log of the sun, where it would be and at what hour, and its angle to the Earth in what season. And come to think of it he must have logged the clouds moving in. He said that the rain always came in from the sea. The clouds moving in were a constant worry. I remember the rain sweeping in, pelting down like stones. That is how it used to be said, the rain is pelting down like stones. He filled many logbooks with rain and its types: showers, sprinkles, deluges, slanted, boulders, sheets, needles, slivers, peppers. Cumulonimbus clouds. Or, nimbostratus clouds. Convection rain and relief rain. Relief rain he wrote in his logbook in his small office, and the rain came in from the sea like pepper, then pebbles, then boulders. It drove into his window and disturbed his logs with its winds and it wet his desk. And he or someone else would say, 'But look at rain!' And someone else would say, 'See what the rain do?' As if the rain were human. Or they would say, 'Don't let that rain come in here.' As if the rain were a creature.

Anyway, my grandfather had a full and thorough record of clouds and their seasons and their violence.

From under the sea a liquid hand would turn a liquid page each eight seconds. This page would make its way to the shore and make its way back. Sometimes pens would wash up onto the beach, long stem-like organic styli. We called them pens; what tree or plant or reef they came from we did not know. But some days the beach at Guaya would be full of these styli just as some nights the beach would be full of blue crabs. Which reminds me now of García Márquez's old man with wings but didn't then as I did not know García Márquez then and our blue crabs had nothing to do with him; it is only now that the crabs in his story have overwhelmed my memory. It is only now that my blue night crabs have overwhelmed his story. Anyway we would take these pens and sign our names, and the names of those we loved, along the length of the beach. Of course these names rubbed out quickly and as fast as we could write them the surf consumed them. And later I learned those pens were *Rhizophora mangle* propagules.

What does this have to do with Borges? Nothing at all. I walked into the library and it was raining rain and my grandfather's logs were there, and the wooden window was open. As soon as I opened the door, down the white steps came the deluge. If I could not read I would have drowned.

Now you are sounding like me, the clerk says. I am you, the author says.

Verso 4 *To Verse, to Turn, to Bend, to plough, a furrow, a row, to turn around, toward, to traverse.*

When I was nine coming home one day from school, I stood at the top of my street and looked down its gentle incline, toward my house obscured by a small bend, taking in the dipping line of the two-bedroom scheme of houses, called Mon Repos, my rest. But there I've strayed too far from the immediate intention. When I was nine coming home from school one day, I stood at the top of my street and knew, and felt, and sensed looking down the gentle incline with the small houses and their hibiscus fences, their rose-bush fences, their ixora fences, their yellow and pink and blue paint washes; the shoemaker on the left upper street, the dressmaker on the lower left and way to the bottom the park and the deep culvert where a boy on a bike pushed me and one of my aunts took a stick to his mother's door. Again when I was nine coming home one day in my brown overall uniform with the white blouse, I stood on the top of my street knowing, coming to know in that instant when the sun was in its four o'clock phase and looking down I could see open windows and doors and front door curtains flying out. I was nine and I stood at the top of the street for no reason except to make the descent of the gentle incline toward my house where I lived with everyone and everything in the world, my sisters and my cousins were with me, we had our book bags and our four o'clock hunger with us and our grandmother and everything we loved in the world were waiting in the yellow-washed house, there was a hibiscus hedge and a buttercup bush and zinnias waiting and for several moments all this seemed to drift toward the past; again when I was nine and stood at the head of my street and looked down the gentle incline toward my house in the four o'clock coming-home sunlight, it came over me that I was not going to live here all my life, that I was going away and never returning some day. A small wind brushed everything or perhaps it did not but afterward I added a small wind because of that convention in movies, but something like a wave of air, or a wave of time passed over the small street or my eyes, and my heart could not believe my observation, a small wind passed over my heart drying it and I didn't descend the gentle incline and go home to my house and my grandmother and tell her what had happened, I didn't enter the house that was washed with yellow distemper that we had painted on the previous Christmas, I didn't enter the house and tell her how frightened I was by the thought I had at the top of our street, the thought of never living there which seemed as if it meant never having existed, or never having known her, I never told her the melancholy I felt or the intrusion the thought represented. I never descended that gentle incline of the street toward my house, the I who I was before that day went another way, she disappeared and became the I that continued on to become who I am. I do not know what became of her, where she went, the former I, who separated once we came to the top of the street and looked down and something like a breeze that would be added later after watching many movies, passed over us. What became of her, the one who gave in so easily or was she so surprised to find that thought that would overwhelm her so, and what made her keep quiet. When I was nine and coming home one day my street changed just as I stood at the top of it and I knew I would never live there again or all my life. The thought altered the afternoon and my life and after that I was in a hurry to leave. There was another consciousness waiting for a little girl to grow up and think future thoughts, waiting for some years to pass and some obligatory life to be lived until I would arrive here. When I was nine I left myself and entered myself. It was at the top of the street, the street was called McGillvray Street, the number was twenty-one, there were zinnias in the front yard and a buttercup bush with milky sticky pistils we used to stick on our faces. After that all the real voices around me became subdued and I was impatient and dissatisfied with everything, I was hurrying to my life and I stood outside of my life. I never arrived at my life, my life became always standing outside of my life and looking down its incline and seeing the houses as if in a daze. It was a breeze, not a wind, a kind of slowing of the air, not a breeze, a suspension of the air when I was nine standing at the top of McGillvray Street about to say something I don't know what and turning about to run down . . . no, my grandmother said never to run pell-mell down the street toward the house as ill-behaved people would, so I was about to say something, to collect my cousins and sisters into an orderly file and to walk down to our hibiscus-fenced house with the yellow outer walls and my whole life inside. A small bit of air took me away.

Verso

My legs, and at the end of my legs were black patent leather shoes. Why is it you only see fragility? Like the wrists of a girl hanging in a mother's hand, or a boy's eyelashes falling on his cheek? Everywhere you see fragility.

Verso 17.2

The dock is. The clerk thinks. Lemon summary, lemon factors. In the lemon distance are lemon wasps in lemon objections. Antipodal green, brindle marrow, marrow's satellite. What are you saying, the author says. Lemon hydrogen, the clerk thinks, insecticides. Lemon files.

We walked and walked and walked in Buenos Aires. At the MALBA you fell in love with Wifredo Lam for the eleventh time. We looked and looked as . . . You always forget him. I never do. Your love is like an annual plant. It dies down and has to be planted again.

Remembered, not planted. As soon as I see *La Lettre* I remember I love Wifredo Lam. The woman is standing with the letter. Her right hand covers her right eye, her left eye is closed, an aquamarine closedness. The letter is held against her body, it covers her right breast. She is nude. The letter is her temporary and secular clothing.

Verso 22 *Latifolius – broadleaved*

This is the truth. The clerk bows her head at this weary subject. She hears the prevarication in that direct object. I lose a lover every ten years or so. I don't know how. A sigh strafes the blue robes of the clerk. Her eyes become dim diamonds. I don't know how.

I went to the Museum of London Docklands on the West India Quay in London. There on the wall there were lists of ships and their cargo during the trade. I was startled to see a name. John Brand, he was the captain of a ship named the *Mentor,* owned by William Lyttelton, and on 5 April 1792, it loaded up in the Gambia with 141 people whom it took as slaves to Dominica. On this wall at the museum there were recorded three more journeys of the *Mentor* captained by John Brand to the Gambia.

When the clerk receives this she asks the author, 'But this is perfectly respectable for the right-hand page. Why burden me with this too?' Yes, the author said but it is so tedious, this type of material is worn out yet it keeps flying around like love flies around in the head, so much debris, brain debris, like the memory of lovers or wives. It repeats without resolution. No one wants to hear about it any more, but it stays in the air. I wake up and it's there, I go to sleep and it's there, I look out on the garden and it is there. It's invisible like the debris around our planet now but it's there, emitting shafts of pink and green light through the atmosphere.

Light? the clerk remarks, I have changing weather, massive storms of many kinds, changeable in any minute. You have loves, you have wives? The clerk thinks about this for a moment. The clerk would like to have loves, would like to have wives, perhaps a small house near the wharf, with a lantern for the evenings, a kerosene lantern with a round filament that puffs and lights when the lantern is pumped. Also a coal pot with a platein from which the smell of unleavened bread would rise; and a book with no writing in it, simply blank pages that the clerk might read and laugh with. She looks at her weathered shoes and her inky hand, her tattered hem.

I've looked for that John Brand but only found another who could and could not be the same; this one was a clergyman and a writer born in Norwich and died in 1808. He wrote a pamphlet called, 'Conscience, an ethical essay'. I cannot find that. The essay or the subject. It would be perfectly normal to write such an essay, whose contents I can only imagine, and still steer a ship to the Gambia, pick up 141 people, and transport them, tethered, to Dominica, returning the profit to Baron Lyttelton. Three times. Three voyages undertaken by John Brand. Yet this could not be he. This John Brand took up a position as rector of St George's in Southwark in 1797.

It's only by chance that you found that on the wall of the sugar museum, you weren't looking, the clerk admonishes, you must be more careful with this collecting of yours. Such an encounter only brings more grief than you can handle. At first with you it is wonder and then it turns into grief, just like your wives. Apparently John Brand was a writer and an antiquarian as well as a reverend; he published a poem, 'On illicit Love. Written among the Ruins of Godstow nunnery, near Oxford', in 1775. You have a lot in common then, the clerk said, going too far.

There was a Thomas Brand, a Whig, who was in the British Parliament at the same time as a William Lyttelton, this Lyttelton was also a Whig and according to *The History of Parliament* was 'listed among the "staunch friends" of the abolition of the slave trade, the subject of his second speech, 16 Mar. 1807.'

Well they would have made their money by then, I suppose, time to launder it in democracy. At any rate, at the moment I can do nothing about this, I need a historian. Because at this point it is ephemera.

I wish this would be over so I can get on with my life, the author says. How long do these centuries last.

As a footnote, hectors the clerk, in 1780 Robbie Burns was on his way to Jamaica to be a bookkeeper on a slave plantation. He published the *Kilmarnock Edition* to sell and to collect funds to enable him to make the voyage. If not for its success . . .

Why are you telling me of this, the author asks. Just to remind you that . . . it is possible that everything is washed in it.

Verso 0.1 *Strophe, turning from one side to the other of the orchestra, the act of turning.*

I would like, therefore, to live in time and not in space. Not the timelessness that is often spoken about but time, in this world, as if living in an area just adjacent to air, a film of air which carries time and where I could be in several impersonations of myself, several but simultaneous. If there were time like this.

But there is time like this. A pause from the author. The clerk lives in time like this, several and simultaneous. The author lives in place and not in time. Weighted. In place. I am always aware of myself in place. There is no universal me. I am specific. I am the critique of the universal, we live distances apart. We negate each other. ■

Boréal

FRENCH-CANADIAN PUBLISHING HOUSE

PROUD PUBLISHER
OF ESTABLISHED WRITERS...

Marie-Claire BLAIS • Michael DELISLE • Jonathan FRANZEN
Louis HAMELIN • Dany LAFERRIÈRE • Lisa MOORE
Alice MUNRO • Michael ONDAATJE • Monique PROULX
Mordecai RICHLER • John SAUL • Gaétan SOUCY
Charles TAYLOR • Miriam TOEWS • Lise TREMBLAY

... AND DISCOVERER OF NEW VOICES

Edem AWUMEY • Virginie BLANCHETTE-DOUCET
Stéphanie FILION • Catherine Eve GROLEAU
Renaud JEAN • Simon ROY
Mauricio SEGURA • Alexandre SOUBLIÈRE

Boréal  *Independent for more than 50 years*

© FRANCISCA PAGEO
Pneuma, 2016

CLOUD SEEDING

Krista Foss

Indra thanks them for arriving underweight. They're just kids, pupils dilated with expectation. She's leaning on a Loza rocket, 'the Super Seeder', petting its pewter bladder with its payload of silver iodide, winking at us as she repeats lines straight out of the 'Cloud Couriers Orientation' document from headquarters.

'We're not sentimental about weather. Can't afford to be,' she says. 'It's not a fairy tale or a mystery. It's a transaction.'

Are these ones beautiful? We look up from our computer screens and lab benches as the trainees file past. Jarilo's fingers go limp on the keyboard. Seth and Feng open their mouths like believers kneeling for wafers. Maya lifts her serious chin. Our judgement is dulled by the arid language from HQ: couriers must weigh under forty-five kilograms; couriers must demonstrate upper-quadrant visual spatial acuity and reflexive problem solving; couriers must open an account into which we transfer payments. (Unsaid: the parents, pimps, guardians and gang leaders who actually get those dollars. Not our concern.) Beauty? We've lost the heart for it.

The new couriers undress for the weigh-in – standard operating procedure. Their naked flesh, its febrile brightness, swallows the hangar's available natural light and pulses it back out. Even the usually effulgent Indra, our ballistics expert, seems greyer next to the arrivals.

'The public veer from anger to despair. And in case you're wondering, despair is more workable for our purposes,' she tells them. There's a bit of a swagger in her walk as she leads them towards the hangar's empty west quadrant. She's wearing shiny army boots; her lipstick's the colour of good bourbon. She hands them thermal skins to don – they have to get used to wearing them. 'Just south of despair is helplessness. Combine helplessness with awe and we're in business. Weather mod exploits helplessness. So we have to be reactive, nimble, fast. That's what we're paid for. We're the gods of this shit. We're invisible.'

The arrivals are silent; the vibe is too serious. Indra cracks a wicked smile.

'Invisible, but cool. Cloud couriers get some fucked-up air.'

There's a high-pitched whirr, metal worrying metal, as the retractable roof exposes an expanse of sky, muscling with clouds. Indra clicks open an umbrella with one hand and holds up her remote weather-maker with the other. The rain falls on cue. It falls hard. Even at the hangar's dry end, we feel pressure systems collide and now it's the kids, six of them, who have their mouths hanging open.

Meteorologists who become weather modifiers all start the same way. Feng, for instance, was eleven. 'Skinny,' he reminds us, as if we'd have a hard time imagining him thus. He lived with his parents near Nansha Beach on Zhujiajian Island. Augusts were insufferable in south-east China. Tourists crowded the shade, sucked on frozen melon Feng sold them, tossing him a few kuai to venture into the sun and snap pictures of the sand sculptures. He slept shirtless. And one night woke to the hut shaking in the dark, the wind drumming sixteenth notes along the walls, seawater and rain spitting at him through an open window. He was flat on the floor when the first wall peeled away and their table pinwheeled through the night air. By the time the bubbling sea met his chin, made his teeth gritty with salt, he was sure he was dead. It was his father's strong grip yanking him up, dragging him inland against the lifting wind and lashing wet that startled him into living. In the morning, numb and exhausted, they went back to the beach to survey the snapped trees and homes flung like a handful of rice against Mount Baishan. Everything became different for Feng in that moment. He was humbled. He was pissed off. Each of us in our six-person cloud-seeding unit tells Feng's story as if it were our own. It is our own.

Indra thinks it's important that the kids fully grasp the technology and understand why pure, irrefutable science is both the product (weather mod) and the spin (Did you see a plane? A contrail? Hear anything? Didn't think so. If there's no evidence we were there, we weren't. A ghost can't be liable.)

'The history of weather modification is an epic of lucky incompetence,' she says. 'Whether it's mixing dry-ice shavings with super-cooled water drops in post-World War II Schenectady or using Tupolev Tu-16s to tag cumuli with paint powder for cloud identification, ours is a science that started with whoops. As in "Whoops, did we just make snow? Did we just cause a sky full of clouds to disappear?"'

Seth feels sorry for the kids when Indra projects a diagram of nucleation on the wall. He makes them each a cup of tea using the propane blaster. All the porcelain mugs have carbon smears on the bottom and the water is too hot. Now they're shivering proto-couriers with burn blisters on the insides of their lips. And Indra's still lecturing.

'They look underfed,' Jarilo whispers. The trick is not to let the couriers get into your head. For instance, don't imagine them in the Wasatch Foothills in May. That's where the pink heat of primrose and the blowy white blossoms of rocky cress can be found. That's where new recruits could misunderstand an avuncular warmth moving in from the west. And we could misunderstand how ready we were.

The first day of orientation makes them believe we're family. After lunch, the hangar roof opens, sun parachutes to the floor and inflates into an acre of light. Jarilo fills a dozen large balloons with a 50/50 oxygen–helium mix and bats them into the air above a figure-eight obstacle course.

'They're clouds! The object is to keep them above you as you cycle around the course. Work together. The only way to win this game is to move as a system, and keep the system moving!'

Liberated from the morning's lectures, the trainees burst onto the course atop lightweight ground bikes, in paroxysms of tricks and glee. Limbs fly out towards the balloons.

'Behind you!'

'Get it! Get it!'

We're pulled from our workstations, drawn to the gumdrop-coloured latex bobbing and circling above the course. The trainees chase and take aim with wrists, feet, foreheads and, in one young boy's case, a very angular nose. They're such hapless goofs, it's hard not to enjoy ourselves. We rarely hear each other laugh this way, forgetting, if only for a moment, that this fun churns data. Graphene and capacitive sensors in the kids' thermal skins collect respiration and heart rates, muscular conduction, caloric output. We cheer and hoot, pretend to be on their team as we make notes: who takes the lead, who falls behind, who integrates with the system, who resists.

We don't have long with a new batch. They're still growing, their shoulders filling out, hip lines curving with flesh, legs getting longer. When they get too big we'll send them back, accounts crammed with an obscene amount of money. Well, most of them. HQ calls it spillage: the thing we lie awake worrying about, convinced the others are asleep.

A yellow balloon drifts away from the formation. Reaching for it, one of the trainees falls off her bike, the underside of her arm sliding along rough cement, ripping open her thermal skin and then her own. We all feel the lamina of that untried flesh buckle then rupture, blood blisters dotting it like pomegranate seeds.

'Got it!' She doesn't flinch. The bike has crashed. She's on her back but the kicked balloon soars upwards. We note the heroic ones. Her name is Rupi.

A long tone signals the schedule change. Rupi is bandaged. The kids move reluctantly to their next training session in the far end of the hangar.

'We're like an effin' junior high,' Maya says later in the lounge while examining her fingernails for dirt that's never there. Mud changed her life – she was across the bay in Rio, writing her first piano theory exam, when the April rains, triple their normal volume, loosed black dirt and detritus from the twenty-year-old landfill upon which the Morro do Bumba shanty town sat. The wall that slammed into the Assemblies of God Church, where her parents and siblings prayed for easier lives, was twelve metres high, an avalanche of decomposition studded with metal and plastic bits. The casualties smelled of rot before their hearts had stopped.

Her voice cracks, deposits its dregs into our chatter. Everybody tolerates Maya, but we resent her squelching what little levity we have. Somebody opens a bottle of Scotch. We ignore a recent missive from HQ – 'Against Empathy: The Importance of Emotional Distance in the Cloud Courier Unit' – and compare the new ones to that other group, the first, the one we can't forget.

'The tallest. He looks like Zack, no? Remember Zack?'

We pretend to have to think about it.

'Like Zack. Jeez, Zack had a story, right? Mum 'n' dad can't grow anything after the river dries up. Flight to the city. Years of running from strafing, bombs. Never knew air that didn't taste like bitumen.'

'Indra lit up like a landing strip around him.'

Maya clears her throat.

'How is SkyBike maintenance going? On schedule?'

'Yeah, good. We're trying out the new ultra-light alloy frames. Paulo, though, right? I sure thought he was funny. Impossible not to smile around that kid.'

'Serena smelled like apricots,' Feng says. It's an open secret he got hung up.

The Scotch does its magic. After an hour we argue about who brought us the most joy from that first group. Hands down Serena, a city girl, thrown out of the house at fourteen, tried the hardest. A few months of couch-surfing, a bit of rough trade: she was existing on tea and cigarettes when the messenger agency found her. Starving herself to bike weight was easy. I was on the plan before they found me, she laughed, her grey-brown eyes avoiding contact. She never got over having her hair shorn. Seriously, how much could it have weighed? No comfort for my fingers now, she said, dragging their tips along the bare stretch from her temples to behind her ears.

Serena was the only one who begged to stay longer, swore up and down she'd stopped growing, that she could out-bike a twelve-year-old, using a voice that was cocky in the upper register, tremulous and beseeching underneath. It's not about the money, she'd say. I got nowhere to go. But all the not-eating made her weak. The SkyBike's oxygen supply is limited; her reflexes became slower. Feng got all testy if someone noticed. Up in the clouds, she began to grip at her handlebars like a rookie rock climber feeling the terrifying suck of gravity. Then came the job in the Wasatch Foothills. After that, our should-she-stay-or-should-she-go argument was moot.

Any idiot can make a cloud precipitate; give a nerd a high-altitude weather-balloon canister of iodide and some open-source calculations and whammo, Granny's got a rain shower for her heirloom tomatoes. But wrangling a weather system – getting it to piss, stop and leave at precisely the right times – that's where our competition was blowing holes into their margins: huge wind turbines, heat lamps the size of soccer fields, an army corps of super-engineered drones worth the gross national product of Uruguay. It was during a Hack-the-Climate weekend that Maya piped up with, What about a kid on a bike? We thought she'd been sniffing the coolant again. Then she pulls out her calculations. Here's how much heat and moisture a forty-five-kilogram kid cycling an ultra-light winged bike at a speed of twenty-five kilometres per hour generates. Stick an oxygen helmet on him or her, integrate a small motor into the bike's crank, redesign the frame for better aerodynamics, put them in a super-conductive thermal skin, then drop him or her into a cloud, and *voilà*! You've got an instantaneous vapour sac, a triggered internal dew point and, best of all, movement; the seeded cloud will cling to the bike like static, said Maya. We radio them directions, they pedal the clouds outta there and find somewhere safe and quiet to land. We go get 'em.

Our jaws hung open. Could it be that easy, that analogue? Seth said aloud the thing we were all thinking: kids are cheap. Even if we paid them ridiculous amounts, our margins would be seismic.

We stayed up for seventy-two hours straight that first weekend, sitting around the 3D modelling station, arguing principles of physics, kinesiology, meteorology. But perhaps not long enough. That's what second and third and fourth chances are for.

Jett volunteers for the trial run. Like Rupi, he's a firecracker. Jett's from Manila; recruiters scooped him up before the drug vigilantes got him. Jett knows how to take a corner on two wheels and not lose speed. Fear is physics' handmaiden, he says.

Wild, what comes out of their mouths.

We release him in low fluff just above the hangar, then circle nervously on the ground. Jett manoeuvres the SkyBike as if he was born to it. 'That's some badass corralling of the altostratus,' says Seth. Even if it's a bit jerky – we see some movement within the cloud's beaded net – the vapour tracks in the right direction. He takes it for another lap; it makes our throats catch, his risking fatigue or using up too much fuel, his showing off. We bend our necks skyward, transfixed.

It takes a while before somebody checks the monitor and sees the hue of violet staining his lips, the darkening moons on his fingernails.

'Coach him down. Coach him down,' Indra yells to Jarilo. 'He needs to land. Now!'

By the time the SkyBike bounces onto the tarmac, Jett's skin is dimpled and blotchy. We can hear the click of his jaw; he's slumped over the handlebars in a palsy of shivers. Indra comes running with a pillow and blanket, undoes his helmet. Seth brings tea. We circle, wring our hands. Maya gets her dead stare. Feng's retching echoes through the whole of the hangar.

We wait until the palest primrose blooms on Jett's cheeks.

'That was killer,' he says with a weak smile. We all take a breath.

But the incident delays production. HQ gets testy. The Wasatch contract was 100 per cent spillage: a disaster. Five years later, we've worked our rate down to a steady 20 per cent. We intensify the ground training and still the recruits are laughing at themselves in spin class, plucking and grooming each other like wolf pups during altitude resistance hikes, pushing their invincible chins against the straps of the SkyBike simulator consoles.

Then it gets serious. We test them at altitude one at a time, for five minutes. We test them in secret – above mountain plateaus, over empty stretches of desert, and chasing stratus along a flooded, burnt coast. We start in low, then drop them into altostratus, altocumuli, cirri. Then we reach upwards into the troposphere – cirrocumuli, cumulonimbi. We test them in pairs. And then for thirty minutes, and then in groups of four for just under an hour. We monitor their breathing, heart rates, brain waves and psycho-emotional fitness. We work out every scenario – rogue winds, pressure changes, plane malfunction, bike malfunction, pedal fatigue, fuel depletion, landing failure – and acquire replacement parts, backup bikes, ejectable flares, ice-nuclei generators. We even very secretly approve two understudy messengers on an as-needed basis. By the time beta is over, everyone looks afraid: them and us.

The truth is we're never going to do better than 20 per cent. Weather mod is the bridle on a mustang; a way of manipulating wildness when you can't eradicate it. What started off as a successful enterprise to enhance the watershed for downstream Utah ranching concerns turned into a chest-thumping spectacle when the Russians and Chinese got into the business. Feng was a solemn youth wearing fatigues, shooting diatomite particles from a repurposed anti-aircraft rocket into the clouds over Beijing so the International Golf Masters Tournament would be bright and rain-free. The Chinese had the numbers – 37,000 rockets alone in a Weather Modification Office. Then Yuri 'The Blizzard' Luzhkov became Moscow's mayor and decided to streamline his annual snow-clearing budget with a little cement-dust cloud dispersal. Jarilo, young then too, was a daredevil pilot and a chemistry ace with an appetite for the Moscow City Duma's under-the-table payments. If Gogol was right that Russia's two problems are roads and fools, at the very least Jarilo helped clear one of them. Until he discovered there was more money to be had elsewhere.

By then weather mod was a fully fledged industry and it was crowded: there were firms promising rain for drought-withered holiday properties, snowcaps restored to super-heated mountain tops, hail diverted from tender-leafed crops and water lapping precisely at dock level in cottage country. It was insane. And the same people who wanted us to staunch the desertification of their suburbs or chase away the rolling fog that delayed their Thanksgiving flights – they weren't ready to hear that there might be, would be, side effects that couldn't always be predicted or contained. Certainly, we weren't telling them loudly enough. Liability stalked us like an old shark smelling blood.

Expel the clouds and they've got to end up somewhere. In China, that was Xinjiang – one December more than 200 centimetres of snow fell. Two toddlers, a father and an ageing auntie froze with bent elbows raised to shield them from their collapsed roof, snow stuffed like eider feathers up nostrils, down throats. When the digging finally reached them, they were frostbite-black; four briquettes of human charcoal.

Above Pereslavl-Zalessky, an armful of 500-grade cement powder used to disperse the winter clouds was clumped into a cinder stalactite and fell to Earth. Even with the drag force – Indra explained – the resulting velocity made the falling cement surgically ruthless. So there wasn't much chance for Petr Youmenko to feel anything at all. He was at an outdoor table eating a boiled egg in one instance, and cleaved perfectly in half in the next. With his right arm still bent holding a fork, his wife Maria, who had sat across from him, swore the eye in the remaining half of his face flickered regretfully at the uneaten egg before the rest of his body crumpled with a sleeping baby's whimper. That such a hard man would end with a soft gush, she wept to her neighbour.

While Sudan dried into dust – there was no money in it – we increased the snow pack for the Wasatch mountain ski operators, extending the season from Provo to Park City well into April. We pushed our luck. 'Shit why not? Let's try for May,' said Seth. And so we did.

It was warm that spring. A thousand metres above the Wasatch resorts, we sent up our Cessna C-172 with 102 silver iodide flares and six nervous couriers, sun-kissed after forty minutes of running around at ground level. Zack had picked a handful of rocky cress, the white petals cloud-pure and as easily bruised as the tender hope that offered them to Serena, a girl for whom tenderness was a trap.

The idea was simple: we'd give the ski operators a little late-season gift on one side of the mountains and get our couriers to take the weather to the other side, where they'd have a soft landing on a plateau beyond the eastern foothills. Jarilo was in the pilot's seat – he seeded a fat and happy cumulonimbus, dropped four couriers into it and another two in the smaller trailing cloud, before crossing over the peaks into the eastern half of the range. Watching from the radar, we could imagine embryonic ice crystals gestating inside that cloud – the body heat of four couriers would torque the process. Sure enough, it started to arc across the sky and forty-five minutes later, a fine dump of Utah powder came down over the peaks and alpine runs necklaced with ski lifts.

But we'd done our job too well: we didn't calculate for abundance. Latent heat from the ice formation, and the exuberance of new couriers on their first job, overinflated the seeded cloud, doubled its output. 'No. No! She's going rogue!' Indra radioed from the ground-level observatory.

The couriers couldn't know it was supersizing, but they knew it wasn't moving. 'Pedal harder!' Seth screamed into their head monitors. The snow kept falling: visibility on the alpine runs diminished. Maya took a call and we could hear a panicky resort operator shouting at her through the receiver. Outside the snow fell and fell. Somebody said the A-word. Indra took off her headset, lay her cheek on the keyboard mumbling that the resorts were alerting their lawyers. 'For fuck's sake, push yourself,' Seth screamed into the couriers' headsets.

They did push themselves. The mother of all cumuli tipped up, and began moving slowly over the range towards the foothills.

Maya was monitoring the couriers' heart and respiration rates. 'Be ready for bad landings,' she radioed to Jarilo who waited on the plateau. 'They're working too hard.'

Within ten minutes the cloud was off the peak, dropping about a thousand feet, before hitting an updraught of warm spring air, and splitting into a big effer of a nimbostratus that started pummelling the highlands with a deluge of rain.

What happened exactly? A convergence of elements we thought we understood: rain, wind and snow. A fraying cloud blocking visibility on one side of the range and exposing May's warm sun on the other. Meltwater and aberrant rains overflowing, creating a valley of roiling water. We think the two in the trailing cloud ran out of fuel trying to get past the foothills. The other four – including Serena and Zack – simply tired out, one by one. They gave everything getting that cloud over the range. Even if they had had the strength to try, there was nowhere to land – they hadn't made it far enough. All six fell out of the sky. One moment, those kids were in the back of the Cessna playing with a fistful of white blossoms and talking about the gear they'd spend their money on, the next they were flat on their backs, eyes facing skyward. And then they were gone. Six underfed bodies, bumping along the bottom of a fast-moving stream, lips and fingertips the colour of gentian, sinking further into the cold hydrological suck of weather.

Nobody sleeps. Not the kids. Not us. HQ has organized a ten-city tour – the itinerary is so dense it might as well be written in Cyrillic. A rock opera of weather.

The first client wants a noon-hour thunderstorm in New York

City. *Thor must hammer his fists,* he wrote right on the purchase order. Asshole. That's code for he's doing something illegal, Indra says. Not our problem, says Maya. Our clouds dazzle and terrify, colliding in a booming celestial gridlock. Then we scatter them; the city cracks open and a runny yolk of sun spills over the avenues. Fifteen minutes is all it takes to distract everyone for several blocks. We're already on the move – the couriers land their SkyBikes on rooftops and Jarilo fetches them with a ground crew.

In Adelaide, the air is so withering that Indra and Jarilo arrive first to cook up a big system over the Flinders Ranges before the couriers chase it towards the city. The rain falls in fat green drops, cooling as aloe to the tanned hide of the land. We can feel the Barossa Valley steam and when the Murray River swells, grown men and women run to its banks and fall to their knees. Rupi and Jett want to stay – give them more, fill the reservoirs and aquifers, they say. But we shake our heads. The client has paid for temporary relief, not environmental remediation (that comes later, at a good price). We don't say that in front of the couriers – we just point to the itinerary and feign powerlessness. At night, we talk in hushed voices.

'We're gods not saints,' says Feng. 'We want people to love us, but they have to be afraid of us too.'

Outside of Timbuktu, we pound the Sahel with hail for a land-banking investment fund based in Hong Kong. We don't stay to see families run into the fields where the golden seed heads of millet have been snapped and shaken, or hear their wails.

'The hail got rid of the locusts, right?' Maya asks as we leave.

'Don't be thick – it's the Fulani farmers we just got rid of,' snaps Jarilo.

And then we're home. The hangar is gaudy with flowers – it smells of jacaranda and white ginger. There are cases of champagne for us, bonuses and expensive clothes, electronics, make-up and fine chocolates for the couriers. Nobody speaks. The kids just want to sleep. Seth's tea is refused. They won't look each other in the eye.

They won't look us in the eye either. They seem older, walking out of the hangar clutching their pay stubs and swag.

Feng opens the first bottle of champagne. There are no glasses so he fills graduated cylinders and hands them out. 'To HQ,' he toasts. 'To us,' we yell in unison before tilting the cylinders back and draining them in one swallow, too fast to enjoy the mineral tickle in our mouths. Feng refills them – again and again, without asking. We drink and drink, because it is there, because we can, because we are tired and have no appetite for words, because we left with six and came back with fewer. Because 20 per cent spillage – roughly, one courier out of every batch – is inevitable, unavoidable.

A moment from that latest tour: somewhere hot, a desert. We were so tired we didn't register the city name. The client – rich, vain – wanted snow for a casino opening. We hired a ground squad so we could throw everything we had at the dry air from above and below. There were so many clouds that we sent up all the couriers, let them choose their favourites. The sky bulged with wild tufts against a Kashmir-blue morning – we told the couriers to linger before they moved the system. The snow fell as if it had been painted. We tried to feel proud. Theirs was such tight work. Except that at this point in the tour, we knew them better: we knew their stories, we'd seen where their nails were chipped, had smelled the vinegar of their breath and heard them whisper meanly behind each other's backs. And we couldn't help ourselves. There was no getting home without spillage. At some point, thinking about the one we would have to lose became thinking about the one we could lose, the one we would want to lose. Secretly, we each made invocations. Please, not her, not him. Let it be that one. We didn't know to whom or what we prayed.

The snow, our best ever, fat and miraculous, fell into our numb hands like fresh white blossoms, veined and supple. We saw the flakes, the intricate crystallization around salts, the purity, and felt terminally, terrifyingly blank. We had done everything so well. Still, nothing could touch us. ■

TWO INDIANS

Falen Johnson

An alley. Downtown Toronto. Late evening. June. The alley walls are covered in graffiti and tags. Milk crates sit in a stack nearby. There are mysterious alley puddles and scraps of garbage everywhere. Two young women enter.

WIN: You do this a lot? Come here?

ROE: Yep. Just about every month. The winter is the best. Snow makes things quieter. Smells less too.

WIN: And how'd you find this place?

ROE: This old Indian guy who used to stop in the store. He came in once looking for a gift for his niece and we got to chatting. He's from up north. James Bay area. He would come in and we would talk. He had these really sad eyes. Looked like he had a rough time, like he had been crying for a long time. Years maybe. We'd talk. Sometimes even have lunch on my break. He told me about this spot. Told me where to find it. Said he felt like there was something special here.

WIN: So how come he isn't here?

ROE: I don't know. I haven't seen him in a while . . . He just stopped coming in.

WIN: Maybe he went home.

[A few beats.]

ROE: Maybe.

WIN: Well you have some interesting hobbies, cousin.

ROE: Come on, have a seat.

WIN: Where?

ROE: Here. [She points to the ground.]

WIN: Ew. No.

ROE: What?

WIN: It's gross. No.

ROE: [She grumbles.] Jesus. Fine. Hold on. [She looks around, goes to a nearby garbage can, pulls out a newspaper and tosses it on the ground.] Sit on his face.

WIN: Holy heck. No. I'd rather sit on the ground. I don't know where he's been. [She points to the politician on the front page.] And that is a bullshit paper. Have you read some of the comments on their website? That's a paper for racists. Racists read that paper. Racists.

ROE: Oh just sit down.

WIN: [She fusses with the newspaper on the ground for too long, looks around. Finds two milk crates. Fusses with them. Dusts her hands off. Picks up newspapers and sets them on top of the crates. Fusses some more. And finally sits.] And now we wait.

ROE: We wait. [She smiles. She sits on a crate.]

WIN: We wait.

[We hear the street.]

ROE: The other day there was this Indian woman in the store. She was the spitting image of Auntie Dana. I thought it was her for a second. Little and brown, cat shirt, yarn poking out of her purse, wearing transition lenses. Just cute you know. And so I was really helping her. Ignoring everyone else in the

store. Helping her more than I help anyone else. And when
she gets up to the counter to pay for her stuff I ask her if she
has a status card and she says, 'No, not on me,' and so I tell
her she can use mine. And she smiles and I go to get my card
from my wallet and –

WIN: Doesn't anyone notice when you do stuff like that?

ROE: No. God no. Most of the people don't even know how to
deal with tax exemption on the computer. There is like
clearly a button. Idiots.

WIN: They just don't know. Lots of people don't.

ROE: No. Trust me. Idiots. You haven't met them.

WIN: Well you gotta teach them.

ROE: I ain't gotta do shit.

WIN: Then they'll never know how to deal with a status card. You
have to teach them.

ROE: Why is that my job? To teach them?

WIN: Because no one else will. You know that. Why would they?
They'd have to see us then.

ROE: Are we talking about the same thing here?

WIN: We are. We have to be the teachers. We do.

ROE: Here we go.

WIN: Not 'here we go'.

ROE: Here we go.

WIN: Okay fine. We don't have to. Then who explains? Then no
one learns anything and we just disappear.

ROE: I'm not going anywhere. And fucking do your own work. It's
not like I came out of the womb with my history written
down in a manual. I had to go looking.

WIN: I know that.

ROE: It's not like it doesn't exist. There is stuff out there. It's not
even hard to find. You just have to do the work. Read an
effing book. Quit asking me to tell you everything in fucking
Coles Notes format. I'm tired of trying to find a metaphor
that adequately encompasses what went down here. Imagine

someone walked into your house and said it was theirs, and then they took your kids away and blah, blah, blah. There isn't a simple way of explaining this. It takes work. It takes undoing. In your own brain. Decolonize yourself.

WIN: Well no one is getting on a boat and going home so I guess we had better find a way to explain their history to them.

ROE: I just wish they would try.

WIN: I think some of them do.

ROE: I think most of them try their best to forget how they are here. Why they are here. What's been built on our backs. Like a few weeks ago there was this powwow right beside work. And I just got a pit in my stomach when I saw them setting up. You know? That feeling when you know you are gonna have to deal with it. The 'here we go' feeling, the 'get ready for it' feeling. And so everybody at work starts bitching and whining about how everyone coming in wants to sit on the patio so they can watch the dancers. One of the guys working the patio actually said to me, 'Hey, wagon burner, you should go do a rain dance so we can close the patio and we can all go home early.' Right to my face. Right to my face with a powwow happening. He was genuinely confused when I got pissed off. I just can't wait for them to catch up any more.

WIN: [She starts to laugh.] Wagon burner. Jesus. That's funny. Wagon burner. What is this, a John Wayne movie?

ROE: I gotta look at that guy almost every day. And he's the boss's son so what can I do? Tell on him? Not if I wanna keep my job. I just feel so angry all the time. Or at least like I'm ready to be angry all the time. Like it is always right there at the door waiting to jump out, almost wanting to jump out.

WIN: I think we all feel like that. Ready to fight. Maybe it's the Mohawk in us. The warrior. Maybe we carry that with us.

ROE: Maybe it's because ten years ago, fuck, five years ago it was all different. No one knew anything and now we have all these white folks lining up to be *allies*. And they look at me with their eyes all big and full of tears and ask me to absolve their ancestors of something and I am sick of explaining it doesn't work that way. You don't get to cry on me.

WIN: Some people wanna help, is that so bad?

ROE: No. Not really. If we know what that means. I just feel apprehensive. Uneasy with all this sudden 'understanding'.

WIN: Maybe you are just used to things being so bad it's hard to feel like they are getting better.

ROE: Are they? Getting better? Because we have an acronym for missing and murdered women? I didn't even know it was a thing. Like I knew it was a thing. I knew we were being killed, I knew this, but somehow I didn't, you know? It's like the schools. We grew up fifteen minutes away from one, drove by it more times than I could count and I didn't know what that building was. I didn't know that our family went there. Because they did so well at hiding it in plain sight from us, they did such a good job of colonizing us that we couldn't see it. I just keep thinking there will be a new headline that explains to me some other atrocity I didn't really know about, or I knew about but I couldn't see. And it will fucking cut right through me. Again.

WIN: Jesus.

ROE: Hallelujah.

WIN: You carry too much. You can't hold all that.

ROE: I'd rather hold it. Try to see it.

[Silence.]

WIN: [She lights a smoke. Exhales.] How's that working out for you?

[They look at each other. Beat. They laugh.]

ROE: I'm just frustrated.

WIN: Oh yeah?

ROE: Shut up. You know what I mean.

WIN: Yeah I do. I just wonder what frustration gets you.

ROE: It makes me fucking care.

WIN: Why don't you just say what you mean?

ROE: Oh come on, we're just shooting the shit.

WIN: Oh come on?

ROE: It's different for you. I don't blame you. You live there.

WIN: You don't blame me?

ROE: I know you know. In some ways. The shitty cellphone signals that drain your battery, you gotta drive half an hour to get groceries, cheap smokes, cheap gas, everybody knows all your business, you'll be able to own a house by the time you're thirty, but you'll never own the land –

WIN: And you think that is the difference? That is what makes here so different from there?

ROE: No, I don't think that is the only thing. I think the apathy is the thing. No one votes or even cares or pays attention to what is happening in the outside world.

WIN: For someone who hasn't been back in years, you certainly think you know a lot about *us*.

ROE: I don't have to go back to know what it's like.

WIN: And now you're all into *foreign* politics. Voting for their government. Taking part in their systems?

ROE: Yeah I voted. I wasn't gonna let that guy in! Fucking dead-eyed soulless zombie. And I wish you would think about voting. Have you even thought about what would have happened if that guy got in?

WIN: You vote down home? For band council?

ROE: Do you?

WIN: I don't believe in that system.

ROE: So you are, what, all traditional now? You Longhouse?

WIN: Of course not.

ROE: Then what are you?

WIN: What am I? I am your cousin. I was there when you fell out
         of that tree house and broke your arm. I was your human
         shield on the way to the bus stop every day between
         kindergarten and grade 12 because you were terrified of the
         dogs. I taught you to inhale a cigarette and how to forge your
         mom's signature. I was there when your dad left and you
         cried and cried. I was there. I was. So why don't you ease up
         and stop shitting all over a place you don't understand any
         more.

ROE: Whoa.

WIN: Whoa? [Beat.] What, you think you're the only one who can
         get pissed off? Who is frustrated every goddamn day? I see it,
         I know it. You're the one who left so stop acting like that is
         someone else's fault.

[Silence.]

ROE: Sheesh.

[Beat.]

ROE: Thanks for teaching me to smoke. It's been really helpful.

WIN: You are such a shit.

[A silence. WIN lights a smoke.]

WIN: You ever think of coming back?

ROE: For what?

WIN: For anything.

ROE: I don't know. I feel more myself here than I ever did there.

WIN: They wish you would. At least to visit.

ROE: I know. I might.

WIN: You *might*?

ROE: I try.

WIN: You try? I don't get it. You have family there.

ROE: Not really.

WIN: Well screw you too.

ROE: You know what I mean.

[WIN is silent.]

ROE: I can't go back there. I know what they think. I know what they see. They can't see me without seeing it.

WIN: Well no one blames you.

ROE: Yeah. I find that hard to believe.

WIN: You blame you. Just because you were in the car doesn't mean you died too.

ROE: You're right. And here, in the city, I can be alive.

WIN: Well. I guess this was for nothing then.

ROE: This?

WIN: [She is silent.]

ROE: This visit? Your big trip to the city as family ambassador to try and make me go back?

WIN: [Silence.]

ROE: What, you didn't think I knew? You are so fucking obvious. Come on. We haven't spoken . . . since . . . hmm . . . let me think. When was that? When was that –

WIN: Jesus. I'm not the enemy here. What is your problem?

ROE: Because I went and because I am the one who left so no one has to try. No one has to care. I left so it's my fault so no one has to call or visit. So if I don't go home, if I don't call then I am the dick. I am the inconsiderate asshole who gave up, who doesn't care, but it's a two-way street. It takes three years for the family ambassador to grace me with an appearance.

WIN: Is this not trying? Sorry but you are just one person. We can't all come running, we have lives too no matter how fucking small they may look to you. Why don't you just go to another rally to feel like you're a part of something?

ROE: It'd be more than you've ever done. At least I try.

WIN: 'Cause you have a medicine wheel button on your backpack? You hold hands with hippies who say they understand us? I see your Facebook pics. Way to go to a rally. Shit, you are trying so hard. Here, why don't you go and make a picket sign with a clever slogan that changes the world. [She tosses the can of spray paint at her.]

ROE: When did you get so mean?

WIN: When did you turn so soft?

ROE: Soft? This is soft? You have no idea what I live every day.

WIN: You're right I have no idea. How could I? You can't even fucking call home to even tell us if you are still alive!

ROE: This is how you get me to go home? By being an asshole? Hey did you think that maybe it wasn't the accident?

WIN: Did I ever think that it wasn't the accident?

ROE: Why I don't come home.

WIN: Oh really, then why? Please enlighten me.

ROE: Because here I get to be me in a bigger way than I could ever there and how could I not like that? And it is such a goddamn mess down there.

WIN: And it isn't here? Look at this place. Look how you live. You live in a basement with no windows. You can barely afford to eat.

ROE: Well at least I can drink the water.

WIN: Oh fuck off, we haven't had to boil in years.

ROE: [She laughs.] Can you hear yourself?

WIN: Nah. I don't buy it. *You are more yourself*? No. You're afraid. And you know what? I get it.

ROE: No. No you don't. You don't get it. You can't. You could never. They are dead and I watched it happen and I am supposed to keep living. You weren't there.

WIN: And there, there it is!

ROE: There what is?

WIN: You are right I wasn't there. You'd prefer it if I was. You'd prefer if it was me instead of Christine or Seth or Ray Anne in that car.

ROE: No! Don't say shit like that. I didn't – I don't want that.

WIN: You guys didn't even want me to come. You never did. I hate bush parties and you all knew that. I was terrible at them. Sat alone somewhere doing my best to not get hit on by some creep, probably related to us, while you guys partied. That night, when you told me there wasn't room in the car, I knew there was. I knew. And I knew that you guys had finally gotten sick of dragging me around. But I didn't care. I got so sick of pretending.

ROE: I . . . I . . . didn't want you to come. I didn't. I am glad we lied to you. I'm glad you are here now.

WIN: I am here and so are you. They died and I learned to live without them but I didn't think I was gonna have to live without you, too. We just want you to visit. It would mean a lot to Grandma.

ROE: Three of her other grandkids are gone because of me. I can't forget that and neither can she.

WIN: Three. Not four. Don't take another one away from her. Don't do that to her. She raised you. You owe her.

ROE: Hey cousin, how come Indians always die in cars? Is it like the new diabetes or something?

WIN: That's not funny.

ROE: It kind of is. Those roads. I know them like the back of my hand. The curves, the bumps, the potholes that come up after the rain. I know them. You know I see them sometimes.

WIN: The roads?

ROE: The cousins.

WIN: You do? Where?

ROE: Wherever it's busy. The street during rush hour downtown, the subway, the mall when I'm on my lunch. I wish I could forget they're dead long enough to really think it's them. To

really give over, you know? I'd like to forget for a few
seconds.

WIN: I saw them once. All three of them in a dream. Right after it
happened.

[Silence.]

ROE: You never told me that.

WIN: I wasn't sure you'd wanna hear it.

ROE: Of course I wanna. I want to now.

WIN: In my dream I woke up on the couch in Grandma's house.
That old grey one. I sat up and looked around for Grandma
and I couldn't see her anywhere but I could hear the clock
ticking. That damn loud clock she has. Tick, tick, tick. And I
could smell something baking. Weird to smell in dreams but
I could. It was cookies or bread or something, something
in the oven. I walked into the kitchen and they were there,
the cousins. They stood at the height chart against the wall
measuring each other to see who had grown the tallest since
they last checked. I don't know why they would. We all
stopped growing a long time ago, but they stood there, Seth
kept going up on his toes and Christine kept yelling at him
to quit cheating, Ray Anne just kept giggling kinda nervous
the way she always did. And they noticed me. All of them at
the same time. And for a second they stood looking at me
and then like a silent agreement between them they grabbed
me and pushed me against the wall. They were laughing and
they were trying to hold me against the wall to measure me.
They kept pushing me and it got really rough and I tried to
get them to let me go but they wouldn't. I got scared and
I didn't know what to do so I yelled, 'You are dead! Leave
me alone! You guys are dead.' And they stopped and backed
away. Then they started laughing even harder than before.
And it got really deep-sounding, not like their voices at all. I

covered my ears and closed my eyes and went to scream but I couldn't. I opened my eyes and they were gone. I was still in the kitchen and I could still smell the cookies or whatever and hear the clock, I could see you and me, but they were gone. I turned and looked at the height chart and their lines weren't there any more. I walked back into the living room and you were there with Grandma. You guys were picking lint off of the carpet in the front room, you both looked at me and smiled and I woke up.

ROE: [Beat.] Wow. What do you think that means?

WIN: I don't know. I don't think it really matters. She still has it you know.

ROE: Has what?

WIN: That damn loud clock.

ROE: I'm not surprised.

WIN: And she still has your grad picture hanging right beside it.

ROE: [Genuine surprise.] Yeah?

WIN: I graduated with honours and yet you still get top billing somehow.

ROE: Sucker. [Beat.] Does she still pick lint off the carpet like that? On her hands and knees?

WIN: Her knees are too bad now. Must bug her. My dad got her a new vacuum but she says it makes her hearing aid ring.

[An ambulance or fire-truck siren, they wait. ROE picks up the spray paint and begins to measure her height. She motions for WIN to come and do the same. She does.]

ROE: Well, I may have top billing beside the clock but you will always be taller.

WIN: At least I have that.

ROE: Remember that time when Ray Anne was just little and she got stuck in the toilet? No one even helped her, everyone just went looking for their cameras.

WIN: Oh God. I love those pictures.

[They both laugh.]

ROE: I miss them so much.
WIN: Every day.
ROE: I don't want to die in a car.
WIN: You won't.
ROE: You can't promise that.
WIN: Well you can't walk through life thinking you're gonna die
        every time you get in a car.
ROE: [She motions to her surroundings.] Public transit, cousin.
WIN: And this is all you want for the rest of your life?
ROE: For now, yes. Hey, you got a smoke?
WIN: Thought you quit.

[WIN pulls out her pack and gives ROE a cigarette. ROE rips it in half
and empties the tobacco out. She motions for WIN to come. She gives
her half the tobacco and walks near the height chart drawing and
looks at her cousin and places the tobacco down. WIN does the same.]

ROE: It ain't ceremonial but it'll have to do.
WIN: It does.

[They take a moment looking at the height chart. The street sounds
in the background grow. It is a streetcar or the sounds of someone
shuffling. WIN wraps her arm around ROE. ROE responds. They stand
watching the moonrise.]

WIN: At least there's still this.
ROE: And we are still here.
WIN: We are. ∎

© LUCILLE CLERC
From *Pour Sûr* (2011), a novel by France Daigle

WHAT IS IT THAT HURTS?

France Daigle

In the Moncton area of New Brunswick where I've lived all my life, we Acadians say it is practically unnecessary to learn English because we catch it effortlessly, like a common cold. If I happen to be listening to songs or reading a book in English, it is natural for me to keep thinking in English for hours, sometimes days, afterwards. Living where English is the majority language, I am constantly making micro-decisions to revert back to French, thereby asserting my cultural origins. But my code-switching apparatus does get tired, and at times the easy way out becomes the only way out. And the easy way out is very often English.

For instance, it made perfect sense to me to write this essay in English rather than French since I am primarily addressing myself to an English readership, but I am certain that if I had written on this subject in French, my starting point and my approach would have been different. This is only natural, I think.

This constant movement between French and English is like the flutter of emotions one may experience on any given day: the emotions may be somewhat annoying or exhausting, or somewhat pleasurable, and within a certain range they are no cause for worry. There is a tipping point, however. There is the comfort zone, and there is the discomfort zone.

F or decades now, I have been trying to understand the role of
language, the impact it had and has on life, on evolution. I am past
the point of accepting expedient or superficial explanations. I do not
adhere to the notion that one's native language – or 'mother tongue',
as we say in French – is some kind of Rock of Gibraltar, creating an
equivalent Mediterranean pool in which one's heart, mind and soul
swim as gracefully as dolphins, drawing some inextinguishable *force*
from this primeval basin so old and deep that this identity can never
be shaken. In fact, I've rather come to suspect that our relationship
to our mother tongue is not primarily sentimental or emotional, but
deeply physiological and that constant and untimely disruptions
and repetitive stresses induced by changing language and cultural
channels cause what could be called a linguistic neurosis. I have no
way to prove this of course, but I certainly wish someone would.

The notion of linguistic neurosis has probably never occurred
to anyone who has not had to function, in any important way, in
a language other than their mother tongue. To them, the concept
would probably be summed up as being 'just a fuss'. Of course, this
perception only serves to feed the neurosis instead of soothe it.

Neurosis usually implies some form of rigidity and as much as I
dislike rigid attitudes, I have also come to embody them. For example,
I very much like the idea of wordless books, especially for children
who cannot yet read. My attention was recently drawn to such a book:
Sidewalk Flowers by JonArno Lawson and Sydney Smith. Praise for
this book was such that I purchased a few copies to give to young
families I knew, plus one copy to keep as a coffee-table book in our
own home. The only problem is the title, which is in English.

Growing up, it was a family principle to always offer birthday,
Christmas and other types of greeting cards in French and where
one could buy such French cards in Moncton became a real problem,
because the vast majority of stores selling English cards did not bother
to carry any in French. For many Acadians, it became a mission to
persist in asking to have an assortment of cards in French. Many
similar demands were expressed concurrently during the 1960s

and 1970s, from greeting cards, books and magazines to catalogues, flyers, telephone services and various official documents. Slowly but surely, an expanding number of Acadians started reminding everyone around them of their existence and their specific language needs – needs which eventually morphed into rights. French schools and colleges, hospitals and many other public services came to embody the extent to which the authorities acknowledged the French Acadian culture.

The publication and production of Antonine Maillet's series of dramatic monologues *La Sagouine* (*The Charwoman*) in 1971 marked a turning point for Acadian French. And in 1979, when Madame Maillet went on to win the Goncourt for her novel *Pélagie-la-Charrette*, it certainly made a lot of us feel acclaimed and recognized, finally, in a big way. And so, literature saves us after all.

Why am I telling you all this? Because to this day, I feel uncomfortable displaying an English-titled book on our coffee table.

The truth: the three copies bought haven't moved from the shelf where I deposited them on the day they were delivered, for even though it is a wordless book, the title sends the wrong message. The wrong message? The message to young children and their parents that it is okay and normal to read English books. The good message is to put a French storybook on the table, even if it has no words in it. So there it is: yes, I am a pusher of French. And in view of the Acadians' habit, perhaps born of necessity at first, of accommodating the English authorities, the fact of standing up for the French language is very often viewed as uncompromising, or rigid.

A t the outset of the Seven Years War (1756–1763), Acadia, with its 10,000 inhabitants, was one of the five territories grouped and known as New France. The other four were Canada (55,000 inhabitants), Louisiana (4,000 inhabitants), Hudson Bay and Newfoundland. Acadia was comprised of New Brunswick, Nova Scotia, Île Saint-Jean (Prince Edward Island), Île Royale (Cape Breton) and Gaspesia. As the British Empire was gaining control over North American territories then under French rule, the Acadian settlements, which mostly dotted the Bay of Fundy area, came to be viewed first as an annoyance, and then, when these French descendants asked the British conqueror to exempt them from swearing an oath of allegiance to the Crown of Great Britain for fear of having to take arms against their own in other settlements, a threat. The English suspected that the situation would become unmanageable and a better solution to the problem was found: the forced removal of Acadians from Grand-Pré and the Minas Basin of Nova Scotia, a large area including south-eastern New Brunswick today.

The Great Upheaval (known as *la Déportation* or *le Grand Dérangement*) was intended to disperse the Acadians in port cities along the New England coast as far as New Orleans, in order to discourage them from regrouping and forming any sort of legitimate identity. And so they were boarded onto ships and their houses, barns and fields set on fire behind them, so as to dampen their desire to ever return. The Great Upheaval was, to put it mildly, disastrous for the Acadians; their population was decimated and their way of life irreparably damaged through shipwrecks, disease, poverty and displacement.

A cadians hung on to their French heritage as best they could after *la Déportation*, in 1755, up to the turbulent 1960s. Of course they had defined and identified as Acadians in the years between, but mostly in a non-provocative manner. There were flare-ups here and there, but mostly the English held the money and the power, and kept things going their way. Acadians learned to bend when there was no other choice and so it is no surprise that the French Acadian language and culture suffered losses through those years. French schooling was minimal and what there was of it remained a constant subject of bickering. Older Acadians remember that it was forbidden to speak French in many workplaces, even well-established and respected Canadian corporations. Consequently, for a very long time, Acadians mostly kept to themselves, earning their living, often with difficulty, from agriculture, forestry and fishing.

It is thus no surprise that twentieth-century Acadian French remained somewhat cloistered in the eighteenth century. The language hardly modernized because most of its *locuteurs* kept on living and working in much the same way as when Acadia was founded. It is true that the establishment, by Catholic congregations, of a dozen or so French-language colleges contributed highly to the evolution of the language as well as to raising awareness of Acadian history and mistreatment, but by the 1960s, when I myself reached the age of reason, many Acadians in the Moncton area were either ashamed of their 'bad' French, or they didn't care much about the language issue because they had other things to worry about.

More than 260 years have passed since the Great Upheaval, which officially lasted eight years. The Acadian people survived and our culture thrives (relatively speaking) to this day. In the last fifty years, officials have expressed regrets and governments have listened to our grievances and have enacted measures to support Acadian culture.

Hanging on to the French language and culture in North America today is no mean feat, especially where there is no critical mass to make the language and the culture sustainable. This, I would say, is what distinguishes the feat of Acadians from that of the Québécois. Lacking an established territory over which we could govern ourselves according to our own needs, the existence of our language has become the ultimate record of our unique history and culture. In other words, our visibility and our affirmation as a people is established through our language. Consequently, any erosion of our French feels like an erosion of identity, an erosion of territory, an erosion of ourselves.

Nearly a dozen historical pockets of French-speaking Acadian communities live on in the Atlantic provinces of Canada today, all cousins to Louisiana's Cajuns, all speaking their particular brand of French. Of these, Chiac is probably the most painful one to come to grips with. This idiom, spoken in the south-eastern area of New Brunswick, where I was born and grew up, is a *mélange* of old and modern French with a generous proportion of English words and syntax thrown into the mix. Chiac is generally viewed as *bad French*, even by us Acadians. Only very recently has it been considered a *demi-mal,* a sort of shield we use to protect ourselves from caving in completely to the omnipresence of the English language.

In our family, Chiac was not encouraged and never written, and if I managed to write six of my books without using Chiac, it is mainly because I avoided all use of dialogue. After each book, I was conscious of having warded off, yet again, the moment when I would have to face the dragon and come to terms with the Chiac dilemma: how could I write dialogue that genuinely represented and reflected my origins and experiences without using Chiac?

At some point in my writing career it was put to me that whatever problem I had or have with Chiac may well be resolved by writing about it, which I have done extensively, especially in my novel *Pour sûr,* published in 2011.

When I did begin to write using Chiac, it was very enjoyable. Here I could feel how I was not simply writing, but truly recreating the sensibility I best knew. The grammatical aspects of writing Chiac were not easy to tackle, and in this I faced the complexities of putting spoken language into written form. For so long I had simply assumed that a spoken language automatically had a textual counterpart. All in all, the experience was both exhilarating and nerve-racking. Breaking the taboo, I felt, demanded an explanation. And then nuances, and then again more explanations. I could not simply throw Chiac out into the world without them. I was conscious of breaking this language taboo, and I did not break it mindlessly. I wanted to give this language issue a good look at.

Today, many years later, I cannot say that my apprehensions have been put to rest. I see there may well be no end to Chiac. It will probably even flourish given its high degree of malleability. But the question is, will Chiac thrive at the expense of French, or will it in fact transform or even replace French? This is a loaded question.

I sometimes think that I am not much of a writer, lacking the depth often born of tragedy. From the start, my specific way of writing – fragmentary skeletal novels – was born of my problem with Chiac and it is mainly by experimenting with structure that I somehow manage to produce books. The mostly young and endearing characters that populate my works seem to have no serious concerns other than this perplexing language question. Can this linguistic tension in one of the world's most civilized countries be considered a tragedy? I suspect that for most readers, it is hardly even a subject of interest. Childhood, family life, community, gender issues, politics, the environment, these are all touched on in my books, yet language is the thorniest subject of all.

I was, like many others, brought up to be made very conscious of our French Acadian roots, and guided, sometimes forcefully, towards all things French. I remember the familiar Grolier encyclopedia and a series of mid-sized vinyl records called *La Ronde des enfants*, a collection of stories for children. Household belongings that some of us seven or eight children would eventually stumble upon and maybe take interest in, in French. There was always this preoccupation, this need to strengthen our connection to the wider French-speaking world. In the 1960s and 1970s, the French language became synonymous with international opportunities, but even for me, blessed with academic abilities and an above-average incentive to learn French correctly, it has not been an easy task. The pressure of English – a universal language, to boot! – is so great that many a French idiom gets lost in the flood.

Nevertheless, as paradoxical as it may seem, I am often dismayed by the poor quality of French I hear around me. My ears are abuzz with errors of all sorts that I would be tempted to blame on sheer laziness or nonchalance. And yes indeed, it hurts to hear French spoken mostly in English. I respect that, for many, language is simply a tool, and Chiac may well be as good a tool as any. Who am I to question? But Chiac does not correspond to the entirety of my identity, and as such I refuse to give it all the room it wants.

In the course of any normal day in Moncton, I often hear English spoken with what I believe is a French Acadian accent. And I am left in awe when, upon my asking, these people tell me that they do not speak French. This has happened to me so many times that I am beginning to think that the anglophones around us have started speaking 'our' brand of English – that the deep French roots of our history have somehow permeated the English language. When I respond by saying that I thought these people were Acadian because they seemed to speak with the Acadian accent, many of them sort of freeze up, or at least show some discomfort. The tear, the rip lies there also, confirming again that something hurts. ■

THE CANADA PICTURES

Douglas Coupland

I'm Canadian. For the first four decades of my life being Canadian wasn't something distinct; to be Canadian was to be a denatured version of being American. Younger Canadians like myself looking for something upon which to hang an identity were offered corny hooks such as, 'A Canadian is someone who knows how to make love in a canoe' – *cringe*.

Dopey platitudes like this stemmed mostly from the one-time-only 1967 Centennial spree of government-funded national-identity-building largesse. Here in 2017 Canada has just celebrated its sesquicentennial with a budget 1/10,000th that of the 1967 celebrations. We did this with a logo that looks like someone's brother-in-law designed it over the weekend. But even so, 1 July 2017 was amazing. It's because as Canadians we know who we are now.

The photos you see here were all shot in two afternoons in 2001. In the year leading up to this I started collecting objects that, in some way, evoked a sense of Canadianness in me, whether they came from my parents' basement, thrift stores, dumpsters or – well, anywhere, just as long as they didn't conform to the flag-waving nationalistic imagery that had been leaf-blowered at me since kindergarten.

When these photos were first exhibited in Toronto in 2002 there was a strong backlash against them – and me – for being so naff as to think that Canadian nationalism merited investigation. *Doug, Canada has been codified and has found its final shape and form. To consider it worthy of further investigation is a joke.*

And then came the internet.

And then came our current world of echo chambers.

And here we are now. Since 2002 Canada has completely reinvented itself. It's become a brand: a sexy, shirtless, vitamin-like, ecotopian and freedom-loving brand. The world's first country with six-pack abs. Canada is goosebumpy *hot*, and what began as a borderline career-destroying body of photos in 2002 now almost seem fusty to me, because in ten minutes Justin Trudeau will be reviving a drowned fawn via mouth-to-mouth resuscitation on Al Jazeera. Afterwards the fawn will lick his nose.

Canada looks pretty on a 16:9 HD screen, but I worry we're getting smug. My mantra since Brexit has been 'Democracy needs morning-after pills', and I think it's true: technology is vastly outstripping our ability to keep up with it. We're one breath away from being led by any of the ever-growing selection of lemons waiting in the wings of Ottawa – throw in a China-triggered plunge in natural resource prices and we're Venezuela with plaid shirts.

But somewhere in these photos lie truths that I hope will withstand the vagaries of the twenty-first-century news cycle. ∎

Kim Fu

Song for Goliath

1

I see them as alpine spruce,
tall sentries on the mountain slopes
that surround a man-made plain, an ugly flat
carved from glacial stone.
(I am the town that gets built there,
McDonald's and an airstrip on pressed gravel.)

I see them standing shoulder to shoulder,
gallant soldiers in a storybook rendering of war,
a ballet about the Imperial Russian Army
that retains the glamorous furs
but empties them of corpses,
blood unfurling as ribbons of silk.
I see them as vertical shafts of light,
squared by trapdoors in a stage.
(I am the phantom between the pilings,
sabotaging chandeliers and young love.)

I see them as portraits of royalty.
I see them sprayed with acrylic.
I see them as a needlepoint sampler,

flowing script that reads: *everyone suffers.*
I see them in black and white on TV,
beaming with the irreproachable, white-toothed
goodness that warms the living rooms of a nation.

2

Our father asked to die at home,
so Rachel tore out the shower doors,
installed grip bars and a new toilet,
cleaned the gutters and the roof.
As she drove us to the hardware store,
we passed a van for a service called
Daughter for a Day. 'What is that?' I asked,
'What we're doing right now?'
'They'd call that "Son for a Day",' she replied, wry.

Rachel crossed two thousand miles of open ocean
in a sailboat, broadcasting coordinates by satellite
so I could zoom out and out on Google Maps,
see a pinpoint in endless blue. Rachel built a cabin
on some cheap land in eastern Washington,
fell while ice climbing and survived by inches.

I said I saw him most in her.
The light eyes and dark skin, straight wiry hair
you could use to suture a field wound.

3

More and more, they are giants and dragons.
I can't see them on the paper-covered bench
at the doctor's, or in their cubicles, or in their urns,
squeezed into the puny, flammable, human world.
I see them hoisting steel beams barehanded,
eating whole cattle sacrificed by villagers,
razing fields and scorching the sky.
I see us having milk and cookies in the kitchen
the night he died. I see us huddled in church
the next morning as strangers sang around us.
And if I must be the bard, then one who tires of
songs about devious underdogs,
admires instead the raw strength of Goliath.

THE FJORD OF ETERNITY

Lisa Moore

The two of them, back in the Toronto office on Spadina Avenue, were rocking the contestable death claims, had doubled the clientele over the last two years, were smoking the competition.

Collisions, Trisha was fond of saying, will always be bread and butter. Scrapes and fender benders. Trisha had started there. But you get bored, and if you have her mobility and her lack of emotional whatever – the way she can hop a cruise ship with two seconds' notice – you start to look elsewhere. Meanwhile, the young guys in the office were all getting hitched and the new wives were, like: Sorry, honey, your cruising days are done.

Not that a fender bender didn't bring in bucks. You get somebody's paint on your fender, you could be talking upwards of seven, eight grand. And enough of those? Karen Kapoor, also in the Spadina office, had uncovered a ring that produced considerable coin for the Russian mafia in Montreal. Busted them because a red Corolla in a parking lot allegedly brushed against the passenger door of a blue Toyota hybrid.

Monetize the kind of dent you can easily pop with a toilet plunger and, next thing you know, you're floating your own paramilitary outfit. Ultimately, though? Vehicle collision? Boring as fuck.

But a good contestable death – that was Trisha or it was Jimmy. The two of them had the Caribbean cruises covered like butter on toast.

Jimmy and Trisha.

What Trisha believed, really? It was Trisha. Not so much Jimmy.

Sure, Jimmy had quaint Father O'Malley jokes that made people feel like nothing was at stake. He talked to men whose bellies sagged over the drawstrings of their swimming briefs and whose sunburnt backs were covered in pelts of curly hair.

Last case Jimmy cracked, he had found himself sidling up to an Albertan raw from a fresh divorce. Fellow named Rusty who had, in the eighties, the foresight to remortgage his Deluxe Executive domicile – 4 & ½ bth, 7 bdrm, two-door garage, marble foyer, wet bar/cedar sauna in the fully developed basement – in order to buy 800 acres and some heifers, all of which he'd sold for ten times as much five years later. He even wrote out a cheque to the divorced wife and kids to whom he didn't owe a dime. But amicable-like, he hands over the big cheque, and his ex bites her knuckle to hold back tears, but she can't, she's slobbering and she has his face squashed between her two palms and kisses him, not passionate, that's so done already, but grateful and bitter-sweet.

Rusty retires early and lives the high life, until the second wife guts him in the next divorce. He loses everything; and next thing you know he's on a cruise and goes over the side of the ship. Rusty wants his twilight years, he wants enough so that he doesn't have to beg for that cheque back from his first wife who, he admits, was always okay with that salon she had – doing cuts and colours, foils and perms, mani-pedis, waxes, massages – and her dozen staff, bewilderingly slothful young women in leggings and long drippy tops, hair dyed like the rainbow, pierced where the flesh is most tender. Sure, Rusty's ex is sitting on a mint, but Rusty has some pride left.

The guy leaves a trail, though, and Jimmy follows a credit card – and look, there's Rusty. Jimmy gloms to his side, and they wigwag their way through waist-deep water to a thatched-roof bar in the middle of the hotel swimming pool in Barbados or St Martin or St Lucia or Jamaica, or wherever Jimmy catches up with him.

So, says Jimmy to Rusty: Father O'Malley walks into a bar and he meets three men, an Albertan, a guy from Toronto and a Newfoundlander.

Here Jimmy hauls out a picture of Rusty from a ziplock baggie tucked into his swimming briefs – gross, Jimmy! – and he smooths out the photo on the bar while they chug back margaritas or mojitos, nearly losing an eye to their miniature umbrellas, and yes, actually, yeah, Rusty admits. It's him. Nearly made it to the Pearly Gates, he says, but instead decided to hole up in a Quonset hut on the beach waiting for the insurance claim to go through.

Alive and well, Jimmy reports to the client. And he's saved Manulife Insurance, what? At least a couple million. Bright and early Monday morning, Jimmy's back in the Spadina office before the tan starts to peel, just as Todd is passing out the day's assignments.

There are a dozen PIs in the company, and who's bringing in the big bucks? It's Jimmy this week. Little round of applause, everyone. Nice work, Jimmy.

The cruise-boat crowd that Trisha and Jimmy work have a mean age of seventy-two. Skin sucked back off their cheekbones like Saran Wrap, the women, smelling of emollients made from aborted lamb foetuses. The men have mostly taken up with younger women and are burning through their pensions before they have to hand over half of it in alimony to their first wives, whose wisdom they miss like a phantom limb.

Some of these guys have COPD so bad they clutch their chests and gasp every time they stand up. A few have colostomy bags tucked into their cargo pants. They've got cameras with lenses that protract the length of their forearms. They spent ten years before retirement brokering manufacturing deals with China for mega-tyres on the high-capacity-haul Caterpillar trucks used in the tar sands of Alberta. Or they developed the waste-water-removal technology for all the major Canadian cities west of Montreal.

During the cruise they'll try anything food-wise, two-fisting it: mammal brains jiggling between chopsticks in the one hand, and the Symbicort puffer in the other.

And Father O'Malley says to the three men, Let's say you've all just died.

The cruise guests disembark on idyllic islands in dense swarms of five hundred or a thousand, collapsing on the beaches like husked molluscs, and Trisha and Jimmy are right there with them, pumping for intel. Trisha and Jimmy flash photos around, and eventually they find somebody who has seen somebody, and these fellow passengers provide a positive ID for the supposed dead guy. Finding these guys is not easy. But Jimmy and Trisha are good.

Trisha would go ahead and say: Very fucking good.

Jimmy has two modes of expression: gregarious wisecracker and sombre truth-seeker. And he reels in the cruise crowd and gets them talking about anyone who looks suspicious.

What does Trisha have? Trisha can do sincerity. She's sincere as fuck. She doesn't get seasick. She's a fast talker, but she listens even faster. It isn't much, but in her humble opinion it puts her streets ahead of Jimmy.

They do the slip traces, make calls to their contacts at the bank, totally violate the so-called dead guy's privacy – so sue me – and track his credit cards and yeah, it's illegal, but please. Don't start. These are the guys who shoot your insurance premiums through the roof.

So yes, Trisha and Jimmy bend a few laws, oil palms while slathered in suntan lotion, live on pineapple and bacon served on toothpicks and a lot of shrimp cocktails. And depending on how patient everybody is, after a while something begins to grow on the widow's wrist back home: a little bling. And soon the bling dwarfs the arm and she's driving a car smaller than her handbag with the top down. Trisha and Jimmy close in.

It was 9 a.m. in the boardroom overlooking Spadina, and Todd slapped down the assignments: one in the Florida Keys; the other, the coast of Labrador and Greenland . . . The coast of what?

Jimmy grabbed the front of his shirt and wafted it open several times in Trisha's direction, a mock gesture that said, Isn't it going to be hot and sexy where he was going? She read the type on the top of her file: The Fjord of Eternity.

What is this? she asked. Fucking Tolkien?

Day-o, me say Day-ay-ay-o, Jimmy sang. He was doing a little hula dance, holding one elbow and swinging the index finger of his other hand in circles like he had a lei on it.

It's not fucking Hawaii, Jimmy. It's a guy dying of asbestos, you dolt.

Eyes like chocolate pudding, Jimmy had.

What he'd said when he met Trisha's girlfriend: I'm available when you gals want to take it to the next level. He'd made fists low, near his waist, and wrenched them back and forth while jutting his hips, twice to the left/twice to the right, mock-wincing with each, you know it, anus pulse, and repeating, Oh yeah, oh yeah. And then a few lines of Loverboy's 'Turn Me Loose'.

So now he'd cornered a file that required going to Key West, camping out in the Holiday Inn, and in the morning driving to the burbs to watch a guy coughing up blood while he puts out the garbage.

Trisha could conjure the whole scene: Why, here's the guy now, coming around the corner of his modest bungalow, and he has to rest. One arm straight out, hand planted on the side of his house like he's trying to hold it up. In the other hand is a garbage bag. He's a few days from suffocating on his phlegm and he's still putting out the garbage? The guy's a mechanic, spent twenty years repairing brakes on Volkswagens in an unventilated garage and he's been breathing airborne asbestos and coughing up big clots of lung tissue. What's he got left? A few days? Maybe he'll make it to the weekend.

And there's Jimmy with takeout sushi, pretentious as fuck, in the front seat of his car, parked across the street, watching to see if maybe the guy is going to light up a cigarette. Because if he lights up, well, there's extenuating circumstances for the lung situation, right? Which we know. Come on, Jimmy. Asbestos killed the guy as surely as if that airborne shit formed itself into a gargoyle and tore into his chest with its fangs.

The mechanic, meanwhile, is doing this last act, heroic and humble. The guy's putting out the garbage before he dies, for the wife and kids. The garbage, like Sisyphus, the garbage, and there's Jimmy with his sushi . . . and personally, Trisha was losing the stomach for that kind of file, so she said: Yeah, give me the fucking Arctic. Todd, give me the Arctic. Give it to me.

In the meantime, she was thinking: Who would pretend to fall off a cruise ship in the great white north? There's nothing for miles except sunshine and icebergs. Not so much as your own shadow to keep you company.

I'll take the Arctic. Damn right I will. Hello, ice cap, here I come. Global warming, give it to me. Reindeer, narwhals, polar bears and shit, I'm on it. Pass me the file, Todd. Do not fucking tarry. Give me your Gore-Tex and the what-do-you-call-them, little microwaveable heating-pad thingies you put in your mitts so you don't lose a digit to frostbite. The file, goddammit. Todd. Give me that mother.

And privately she was thinking: Huh? This guy went overboard in polar bear country? Name of Loveys. Some kind of rock musician. On her computer, Trisha flicked through photographs, hordes of people in stadiums all over the country holding up BIC lighters, swaying, and this Loveys dressed all in white with the backstage lights blazing around him in a halo. Married six times, kids with all six, dozens of grandchildren.

Next she was on the phone to Roy at OptiLife: I'll cost it out for you. Roy, you're looking at twelve hours a day at one-fifty an hour, the cost of the cruise, which is hefty, and add an isolation fee.

A what?

Isolation fee, Roy. Northern isolation fee.

It's a cruise ship, what isolation?

Roy, you with me?

I'm just trying to follow isolation fee.

Then Roy said something mushy about the seal hunt.

Let me ask you something, Roy, Trisha said. You wear leather shoes?

Those seals are babies, Roy insisted.

They haven't taken the babies in years. Check your privilege, man.

Helpless, bawling adult seals, then, looking up with those big black eyes.

You know they're designing chickens now that are all breast, right? They don't even have legs. In cages, they can't even shift their weight. They can't move at all, Roy. Breasts with little brains, brains just big enough to register, Hey, I can't shift my weight. You eat chicken, Roy? A little cordon bleu s'il vous fucking plaît?

She costed it out to thirty thou and then gave him what she called a deal at twenty-five. Because, she said: I like you, Roy. You're wrong as fuck, but you have convictions. Loveys is alive and well. I'm going to hunt him down.

Thanks, Trish. You have a good reputation, he said. He sounded chastened and maybe smitten.

I don't like to toot my own.

One thing, he said. Loveys. That man's beloved.

What are you telling me?

Beloved.

It turned out there were no cabins left on the ship to the Fjord of Eternity because it was one of those cruises that catered to a better sort of clientele. They only accepted a couple of hundred customers and the passengers listened to lectures on sea mammals and anthropology during the bad weather. So the guy running the ship said, We'll hire you as a sales rep. Trisha figured there was no need to tell Roy she was double-dipping.

And that was why she now found herself in the staffroom, digging through Tupperware containers full of costumes for the *Explorer*'s Night Variety Show.

Trisha jammed a Viking helmet with walrus tusks and blonde braids on her head. She dragged a plastic sword out of the tickle trunk like it was Excalibur.

It's all Viking crap, another sales rep, Selma, was saying.

Staff can't all be Vikings, Chloe said. Chloe and her partner Chad were aerialists who performed from a hoop that swung out over the side of the ship and turned on a swivel. They sat on the hoop like it was a moon, shifting slowly under the stars, and over the reflection of the stars on the night water. They would affect a lovers' quarrel, and Chloe would let herself slip off the hoop and drop, only to be caught by Chad's big toe. Their feet locked together, he would hold her over that black void full of starlit squid ink. Her arms hanging down towards the waves, a bone-crushing distance below. But Chad would draw her back up into the hoop and then they'd air-kiss each other's cheeks and throw their arms up: Ta-dah!

Chad and Chloe had a newborn infant girl who had been thrust into Trisha's arms just before their last performance. Trisha had watched them swivelling and swinging, peeking between the fingers of one hand clamped over her eyes while jostling baby Jasmine on her chest. When Chloe came back on deck she popped a boob out of her rhinestone-encrusted Lycra, and told Chad to get the diaper bag.

Here in the staffroom, getting ready for the costume parade, Chloe was all business. She was trying on the helmets and tossing them to the side.

Were you on this trip last year? Trisha asked. Remember a guy named Brad Loveys?

Remember him? Chloe said. I'll remember him all my life. Where do you think Jasmine got those green eyes?

Her eyes are green?

Green eyes.

So you and he?

And Chad.

You and he and Chad?

Loveys was something else.

The three of you?

A threesome.

And it was good?

Me and Chad, we're the ones who spray-painted his guitar gold.

So, Loveys was alive?

Was he ever!

Somebody should be Franklin, Yolanda, the staff archaeologist, said. She dug through the pirate eyepatches, synthetic beard/moustache sets, kerchiefs and wigs.

Bingo, said Dave, as he put on a puffy chef's hat. Dave was a seabird specialist and had a zodiac licence.

Captain Cook! Selma said. Someone get a spatula from the galley.

Trisha watched this scene, still gobsmacked. She had discovered something hitherto unknown: Loveys might be a true goner. If so, he would be the first one since she signed on to be a PI five years before, at the age of twenty-three. Here's what she knew to be true: Loveys had jumped. And he'd survived the hypothermia, a miracle in itself. She'd already, earlier in the cruise, followed his trail through tiny communities in Labrador, where he'd played to sold-out bars, and other communities of 250 people where flayed seals were kept fresh in the waves near the wharf and the people came out to meet ship's passengers with flummies and bakeapple jam, drumming on bodhráns and singing Haydn hymns brought to the Arctic by the Moravians, but translated into Inuktitut. She'd showed Loveys' picture around, and everyone had told stories about his guitar. The guitar was gold.

And the music.

Okay, it was nothing short of transformative, this music, and it had altered the very cells in their bodies and minds. They were united and inarticulate about Loveys' music, except to say that they were forever altered. They mentioned how he was just sinew when he played that guitar; he was made of rubber and sticks. Elbows like boomerangs and his middle was a slingshot with the guitar as a stone he was trying to hold back. The alcohol and the crack had carved away most of his flesh. His eyes, they said, were like the Northern Lights, that very shade of green. And he had no eyebrows. And how virile he was.

Insurance fraud of the sort Trisha investigated involved perps who were dentists with erectile malfunction, men who were scarfing antidepressants and hit a wall. People who refused to accept that they were finite and succumb to the seismic shit-show of horror/joy that amounts to getting ready for the . . . what did they call it now? The third act.

Loveys didn't fit the profile.

Loveys was a torch song from the get-go. He was a blast of rage and equanimity, a one-man cult, a rock star in a tinsel wig and rhinestones. Crackhead, raconteur. Teeth like Stonehenge, but the smile? Sly and sensitive. The eyes, we've already heard. The eyes were what people kept talking about. Not tall, but boots with heels. Not averse to make-up for television and stage. Did he swing both ways? Think pendulum. Shot out of the womb a few months early, couldn't stand to be confined.

What had Trisha gathered?

He had tried to go clean before the cruise. He had tried to give the crack the shake, but the crack shook back. The hold was too strong for poor Loveys. He'd poured all his bottles down the sink and gunned his truck to an abandoned community back in Newfoundland, with nothing but a cooler full of Vienna sausages, and then he'd slashed the tyres of his truck so he'd be stuck until the DTs passed.

But when the shakes set in he drove on the wheel rims back to town, sparks flying in all directions. The gas tank caught and the thing blew, spinning out on the arterial like a Catherine wheel, cars squealing to the left and right until Loveys' truck came to a stop.

Close to a whole minute later, spectators said, the door on the driver's side flew open and he got out with his guitar, his back aflame, giant wings flying up towards the heavens from his shoulders.

Loveys took off his jacket and left it burning on the asphalt, got a ride back to town with his burnt-off eyebrows still smoking, cuddled the bar at the Barnacle and played for two weeks straight. People said he didn't go home. Slept on the bar stool.

All the other bars downtown emptied out and the summer crowd packed themselves into the Barnacle to hear him because the music had everything in it, all the anguish Brad Loveys had ever felt: how he loved his family with such fierce intensity it gave him a stomach ulcer, especially his departed mother. He'd done everything for his mother, who had died up on the Northern Peninsula and been laid out in a pine box that Loveys had hammered together himself.

She'd been waked in the living room with its display of miniature Red Rose Tea figurines – lions, sea walruses – marching across the mantle and a crocheted blanket of lime-green and orange Phentex wool squares flung over the foot of the coffin, and there'd been no embalming or anything.

In his mother's last moments Loveys had had two fingers on her neck, feeling the pulse banging away hard until it got faint and then he couldn't feel it at all. Then he took his mother's face in both his hands and touched his forehead to hers and his tears splashed off his own cheeks onto her face, and because she was gone away to nothing the tears slid fast over the bones in her cheeks and down onto the pillow. He dragged the guitar out and sang, more howl than song, right there beside the coffin.

A week later, her employer called – she had been a social worker, child protection – and said how insurance would pay for the funeral. And he'd told the truth: there had been no expenses but for a few sandwiches with the crusts cut off for people who came by, and the lobster in them sandwiches, which he caught himself. But the cheque still came and paid for a two-week bender, and this is when he got the idea about jumping off the ship. Insurance companies were giving money away.

Loveys' dead mother appeared when he was trying to dry out and told him to keep on playing. That was what he had been put on Earth for, according to Mom Loveys.

She said all this without moving her lips. Loveys' mom had appeared to him as if encased in a milky and semi-opaque envelope floating two feet off the ground without a stitch of clothes, breasts down to her belly button, broad across the hips, three rolls of belly and the short little legs which Loveys had inherited, but all of it transparent (he could see the heart and lungs and the bowels, small and large intestines, even a clump of stool that hadn't made it out before she had died, the prune-like ovaries and the womb, for which he'd felt a pang of nostalgia). More importantly, inside her there was a constellation of stars, which Loveys understood to be radiating love, just love.

So there he was at the Barnacle, for two weeks before he boarded the cruise ship, singing and playing the guitar. The songs told about his old mother, but they also spoke of the lovemaking he had engaged in over a lifetime. They evoked a young woman with rollerblades on new asphalt, and the rumble of those blades, her lime popsicle and her cold mouth when he kissed her – and this was his first wife. And he sang about each of his wives and his children, how their hair had smelled when they were infants, and the mustard colour of their infant poo, and his dog that shed white hair all over the couches and was hit by a car, and whom he'd found in a puddle after a thunderstorm and torrential rain and a whole night of searching for him, and how a bone in the dog's leg had stuck out, and how the vet sewed him up and how later, years later, the vet put the dog down and the dog died with his eyes open and Loveys asked the vet to close them and the vet said it couldn't be done. You can't close a dead dog's eyes. Loveys sang about never being able to close your eyes.

People were pressed into the doorway of the Barnacle and blocking the sidewalk and spilling out onto the street, threatening to trample each other, trying to get closer to the source of that music. Loveys sang about everything from genesis to eternity, and the cops showed up because the hullabaloo was blocking traffic, and they, too, got out of their cars, which they'd left parked slantwise across the road, and stood still, listening along with the crowd.

Now Trisha was down in the bowels of the ship with staff from all over the world – Ghana, Guatemala, the Philippines and Nicaragua, El Salvador and South Africa. Some of them had not been home for nine months or more, some of them had babies they had never seen, babies who had been born back home while these staff cruised from place to place, swabbing decks, sous-chefing, or turning down bedding. All these men and women were here, grinding on the dance floor.

They started a party game, with the men in a circle facing out, legs squeezed tight together so they could hold up a carrot, an orange stick jutting out from their crotches, how lewd and marvellous; there were strobe lights and streamers and women doing the rumba in a circle around the men, dancing hard to taped music because they couldn't stream a note.

They were nine miles into the fjord and had left the rest of the world behind. There was no signal, no internet, nothing. Just glaciers out there in the dark, the ice demurely drawing back, everything vulnerable and lost at the top of the world.

When the music stopped, the women had to grab at the carrots, snatch them from the men's crotches, and squeal with electrified joy if they were successful. Whoever didn't get a carrot had to make out with a carrot-castrated man, and chug a beer with him and crunch the can.

Trisha didn't get the carrot because, really, she couldn't make herself grab there – it was a man's crotch, for gosh sake. So she kissed this guy, joining tongues and hands – a guy with a synthetic beard down to his belly button and a wig from the Tupperware costume box, and she's not even into men, she tried to tell him. But she still couldn't get enough. Who are you?

He said: Omelette Station, Omelette Station! He didn't speak English: those were the only words he could say with confidence, and sure enough, she saw him the next morning, both of them hung-over as hell and shy-smirking at each other – some onions please, and Cheddar, yes – as he made personalized omelettes at the breakfast banquet in the upper-floor dining room.

But all that came after she staggered back to her cabin, the ship rolling such as she had never experienced before. She just made it to the toilet, and what happened there was so violent she knocked her contact lens out. Her very soul is what she vomited into the crapper, and there was a strange vibration in her butt as she hugged the toilet bowl, hugged that bastard like it was her lover. It took her a moment to understand – she'd pocket-dialled Jimmy from the Fjord of Eternity, where you can't get reception . . . but never mind, she had reception.

Jimmy? That you, Jimmy? It turned out Jimmy was at the stake-out with his sushi in the Florida Keys, raw tuna and seaweed, and his guy was there with the fucking garbage. This guy, said Jimmy. The blood from his mouth and nostrils, gushes of it spurted, because of the asbestos in his lungs, and out came his two little kids, to whom the guy says, Back in the house now kids, Daddy's gonna be fine. And Jimmy dropped a tuna chunk from the chopsticks and it went down the front of his shirt even as his tongue wriggled out to catch it.

The guy, Jimmy's guy, at that very moment he patted his chest pockets and what do you know: out came the pack of smokes. Jimmy went for the camera, click-click-click.

Got him, Trisha, he whispered. Fucking got the bastard. Ka-ching. Fucking ka-ching. And that's when Trisha lost him. The signal was gone as fast as she had happened upon it. Jimmy? Jimmy? Trisha spewed some more.

She would tell Roy at OptiLife everything: that she had failed in her mission; that she'd seen some things on the way. She would give up her cubicle on Spadina and would never again have to watch Jimmy with a fleck of couscous on his cheek from the jumbo wrap with shredded lettuce, falafel and sriracha; never again hear him ask: could she pick up one for him if she was going to that little place on the corner, I mean if she was going anyway? Could she spot him? He's good for it.

And she would never leave the Arctic, because the sublime had broken her. And if Roy of OptiLife knew what was good for him, he would leave his job, Roy, and come on up here to see for yourself what she was talking about.

Once she got internet again, she would tell him. In the meantime, before bed, she would go on deck to tilt her face towards the midnight sun.

When Trisha caught up with Brad Loveys, she was on the third deck, starboard side, of the *Northern Explorer*. The crack in the cliff where Loveys stood was as wide as a six-lane highway and full of glacial spill. There had been no sign of human habitation for maybe seven hours. They'd been going ten knots most of the night.

Just mountains on both sides of the vessel. Behind Loveys there was nothing but nowhere, and lots of it.

The Fjord of Eternity at his feet.

He stood with his legs apart, his wig of blue tinsel full of static electricity and the luminous strands raised all over his head like a flame from a propane torch. The midnight sun searing his gold guitar. From the deck of the cruise ship, the guitar seemed to writhe. A trick of light and oblique angles made the neck look like a snake he was holding by the throat. Loveys' body jackknifed back and forth as he tried to hang on to it. He was clinging on for all he was worth. Sometimes he leaned so far back under the wriggling instrument, his crotch was pumping towards the sky and his shoulder blades came close to the ice rubble behind him.

The light at that hour was Bubblicious pink and Orange Crush orange and hazard-tape yellow and it was pixelated in the haze rising from the water, brackish and old-fridge-smelling.

Trisha thought about how she had cruised the coast of Newfoundland, through Iceberg Alley, and on up to Labrador and disembarked on Cut Throat Island, where the bear monitors in fluorescent orange vests spread across the hills. It was possible that Loveys might have stayed there for a winter, but when Trisha and the other passengers had stepped on the beach and seen paw prints, big as your face, still filling up with water, like little finger bowls, claws clearly delineated and steaming scat, it seemed more likely that Loveys' shin bone would have made a toothpick for some peckish polar.

They'd stopped in Hebron and Ramah, resettled communities where they were told not to step on the sunken sod houses. The struts would have been whalebone, Yolanda, the staff archaeologist, told passengers, and the windows translucent seal intestine, and the floors shale. Storms, and babies born and blubber shared, all lit up by a soapstone dish full of seal oil and a grass wick.

Trisha had flashed Loveys' photograph around to the six archaeologists marooned from Memorial University for the summer, swollen beyond recognition with blackfly bites. They'd set up camp in the Torngats, armed with their camel-hair brushes, magnifying glasses and ball-peen hammers.

A young woman, Brittany, with a post-doc had said: Yeah. I've seen him.

Craggy-looking?

Craggy, yeah.

Eyebrows?

No eyebrows.

But something enigmatic?

Sexy.

What was it?

His eyes.

He has nice eyes, you're saying.

Yeah, unnaturally green, with tug.

Tug?

They tug you right out of yourself.

You're saying . . . ?

You can't look away.

Are you saying something occurred between him and you?

Absolutely.

So, he was alive?

He was very fucking much alive.

But by the time Trisha spotted Brad Loveys on the green-grey, blue-grey 10,000-year-old glacial spill at the top of the world, about to be devoured by a serpent/guitar in the Fjord of Eternity with nothing for a million miles in any direction except silence, she was convinced he was dead as a doornail. That's what she'd be telling Roy and Todd, and all the guys she'd ever have to answer to, for the rest of her life.

She raised her hand and wiggled her fingers hello. Then the ship cruised past the wall of ice and the crevice closed shut.

Dead and gone.

Except, she still heard the music. ■

The stunning new novel from the author of *The Vegetarian*, winner of the 2016 Man Booker International Prize

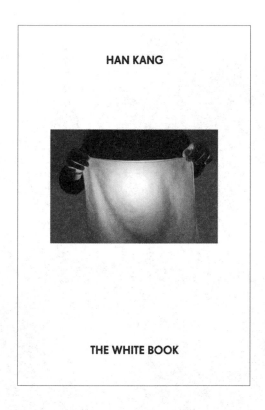

www.hankangwhitebook.com

NOVEMBER 2017
978 1 84627 729 3 | B FT HARDBACK

www.portobellobooks.com

/ portobellobooks.com

Portobello Books

Manawan, 2017
Courtesy of the author

TSHINANU

Naomi Fontaine

TRANSLATED FROM THE FRENCH BY DAVID HOMEL

Knowing your words

The train is packed. Children are running up and down the narrow corridor between the rows of seats facing each other. The youngest are lying on the thick upholstery, sleeping tight, their breathing soft. The older ones are playing cards on the fold-out tables. I hear laughter and the familiar language of the hunt. Outside it is winter and the north wind shakes the trees heavy with snow. In the warmth of the train car, we talk about this and that, we don't need to say too much. I'm eleven years old.

You're sitting across from me. You're watching the forest move past. You're elderly. Maybe a little too old to be taking this long day trip. You're spending less time in the woods now because your bones have started aching. White hair, eyes like slits. Skin tanned by age. The wrinkles on your face, abrasions or history. You are talking to me, murmuring in a distant language. Your hands tremble ever so slightly when you point to the woods, the mountains, Nutshimit, the land in the centre. I don't know what you're trying to tell me. I can hardly understand your gestures and misty eyes. I listen. I watch you carefully, and it's not easy, but little by little a wall breaks down.

I wish I knew your words. I would write them down and store

them in my memory, the way we keep life inside us. The way we have our strength when we face uncertainty. I wish I knew the things you are speaking of, if only abstractly, without having touched them, but seeing them with your eyes.

It's like making the journey the first time. Great spruce covered in thick snow. I look into the distance, the bluish line of the horizon. The slow continuum of a wild landscape, unaltered. I know all of this is perfect. In your mind, grown tired with the years, maybe you are trying to bequeath your memory to me. Maybe there is another way behind your purity. Rougher, with more hazards, harder to preserve from ignorance. Perhaps you know where that road leads.

Later, they will tell me you were a great man. A man who knew much. A scholar of the hunt. An expert in the art of the drum. A prophet when it came to recognizing the rights of the Innu. A human dictionary, they will tell me. They will say that to me. Because, with the words I did not understand, I will want to write your life. Nimushum, my grandfather.

Returning

Returning is inevitable. In this tiny village, in this setting of thorn and sand, constructed in my imagination since childhood, I have immutable memories.

On my street, I blended in, a quiet little girl. When I was a baby I cried so rarely that my mother would shake me awake to make sure I was still breathing. When I was a child I was so quiet that once my mother forgot me on the steps outside. Later, the strange justice of life caught up with each of her tears.

When I left my beige-coloured house with the dark-brown beams, I left everything. Everything might not seem like much when you own almost nothing. An iron bedstead and a cover with a beige-and-white leaf pattern. A doll's house, an enormous playroom in the basement. Spending the winters with cheeks reddened by the cold, and during the summer, my skin as dark as children from the South. Maybe one day

I'll return to the shores of the bay, kiss my aunt and go play in my room.

Exile is an eight-hour drive and it has pale skin. My mother needed two days to make the trip, a distance I calculated by the number of villages we passed through. I ended up knowing their names by heart. And the stops, and the stages. Keeping the pace, moving at the speed limit. I don't know if the world has changed elsewhere, but I do know the deadly curve at Saint-Siméon that they finally replaced with a straightaway. And the bridge that was never built between Baie-Sainte-Catherine and Tadoussac, the riverbed as deep as the sea. And the tiny parish whose name I have forgotten, that will soon close down now that Route 138 has detoured around it.

They say return is the path of all exiles. That in a person's patience there is an end to the isolation they have lived. I didn't choose to leave. Twenty years later, I return and see that things have changed.

Innu-aimun

L anguage is a risk that a nation takes. If a language survives, its people do too. If it is drowned, the people drown. I have two languages, French and Innu, but only one is mine. Because my grandmother will know I am talking about her if I say 'Nukum'. Because my son understands that 'Nekuess' is also his name. Because the deep love I have for those dear to me is spoken this way: *tshe shuenemeten*.

What's risky in this bet is free will. A professor of the history of French told me that it takes three generations for a language to be lost in an immigrant family. If the grandparents are unilingual Spanish, for example, the parents will be bilingual Spanish-French, and the children will speak only French. I'm not an immigrant, but I live in a city where no one speaks my language. I am carrying on that battle, and I'm not the only one. Our children must not be the last generation.

I want my son to learn to say 'Neka' when he has something very important to ask me. I want that closeness, like a secret, when we speak Innu together in public. I want him to understand his young cousins from Uashat when he plays soldier in the middle of the street. I want an age-old root to remain inside him. What a great burden for a little man who is just stammering out his first words!

Nuta, my father

My grandmother writes to me on Facebook, short messages filled with mistakes and love. She wants to tell me that it's my father's birthday. He would have been forty-six. She tells me she misses him a little every day, and on this sad occasion, her thoughts fly one by one up towards the sky. Nothing in my memory can help me remember that dark-skinned man with his Indian beauty. Nothing that could fly high, very high, towards the sky. Except this one thing.

And that's a photo I keep in a blue suitcase that is much older than me. A picture of him in khaki-coloured winter clothes, a rifle slung over his back. He is wearing a cap that looks like part of an army uniform. He never was a soldier or a sharpshooter – just a hunter during the prime of his life. One knee bent, holding a lynx in his hand. The blood staining the snow proves his success. Brown eyes, mouth set, a straight nose, tiny freckles on his cheeks. He's handsome. In his twenties, no more.

The photo is supernatural. Death looks like nothing, only an image empty of memory. He is dead only for those who knew him. For the rest, he will always be a hunter, a young husband, a father proudly posing with his firstborn son in his arms. A few ageing pictures, my heritage.

Happy birthday, Dad.

Neka

Soon, while we are still curious and single, I will take you on a trip to Europe. You will overcome your fear of flying and heights and plane crashes, like the ones you see in the movies, and you will settle for the tiny portions the flight attendants serve. I'll take you to see the Eiffel Tower and the Champs-Élysées that has nothing in common with the roads in Quebec. That will remind you of the song that played over and over in the car when we went out in the evening to look at the Christmas lights. We will have time to eat slowly in restaurants, the prices of which will be beyond our means. I will take pictures of you by the Seine. We will visit castles, two princesses in search of their Prince Charming. The best champagne will grace our table, and coffee that is much too strong, and which you will dilute with warm water, naturally. The shop windows and the old buildings and the men's accents will impress us. Midnight in Paris is hardly midnight in Uashat. And then, maybe because of fatigue and the long walks, we will cry. But they will be tears of joy.

When I step onto the stage, I'll talk about you. As all those researchers and writers and professors look on, I'll say that I'm proud to be your daughter. And that dreams, ambitions and talent flourish more easily in a happy childhood. The kind of childhood that helped me learn to trust in life. *Tshi nishkumitin*, Neka.

Tshinanu, us together

O f course we are different. We speak a language that is foreign to you, though sometimes we stray into yours to name modern objects and digital spaces. We live in villages that other people call reserves, but if you knew the language you would understand that we inhabit the territory. Of course our houses are made of wood and cement pushed into the earth. Our facades are not brick. Our fences are never solid enough for those who have travelled long distances. Nor our hearths warm enough for those in constant need of a pat on the back. Closeness has nourished us, raised us, turned us into men and women. We are the people of the North.

Of course the children's eyes shine the way they do everywhere else, they light up at the pleasure of soft ice cream or an afternoon by the water. These children grow up and of course, when they

become adults, they try to find their way. Sometimes they lose it.
Then find themselves once more. And, of course, we live on sand.
By the water and the lakes. We bathe our thirsty bodies one month
out of the year, when the sun offers us its heat. The horizon we look
to offers us infinity, a dream. Of course the women yell at their men,
and punish them for their infidelity. Then they forgive the fathers of
their children. Of course we like our beer and wine, quiet drinks and
soft music. The evenings go on forever, we dance through the night.
Of course we die and we are born. We lament and we pray. We marry
for life. We love and we promise. We hope. We dream. Of course, we
are different.

Weekend

Friday, four in the afternoon, my bag is packed. Chips and soft
drinks, clothing that's warm and comfortable, no make-up, no
perfume, rubber bands and a toothbrush. My uncle finishes loading
the pickup. I go into the house to talk to my aunt. I have a problematic
student who is driving me crazy. I feel like I've lost all control with
him. She tells me he's the son of so-and-so. She knows all about his
mother who ran off with her Schefferville lover.

Two hours' drive. Old country songs from an Innu group. We
smoke cigarettes like a couple of chimneys, my aunt and I. Stopping
for coffee in Port-Cartier. The gravel road you can never take your
eyes off in case there's a porcupine. The trees that grow one on top of
the other and the streams that separate them. Autumn isn't red and
orange like it is in the South. It is dark green with yellow spots. I think
of the anger I feel towards my student again. I understand his a little
more. Two partridges killed by the roadside: one in the head, the other
in the belly. My aim is better when my uncle isn't watching me.

Pine and spruce grow close to the cottage. A few birch, small trees
with yellow foliage. The lake where my grandfather built his cabin
stretches from one end of the horizon to the other. Taking the canoe,
I can reach other families, other hunters. Years later, my aunts built

their cottages near the cabin. There are five of them in all, like a small village. Along the shore, there is a peninsula where grey tree trunks are drowning. At first sight, you'd think it was a moose going for a swim. You look closer, then call off the urge to alert a hunter. It's not impossible, but you just have to be aware.

From the big window, you can see the lake from the cottage. Coffee tastes better here. It was cold last night, and I slip on a heavy wool sweater while my uncle puts a log in the wood stove. He asks me if I was cold. I say yes, a little. He'll talk about it all weekend, and make fun of me when he fills the stove before going to bed. I laugh along with him.

Dissatisfaction gives way to simplicity. You don't look at yourself in the mirror. You look at a crystal lake, watching for the circles that trout send up from deep in the water. We drink from the stream and don't throw anything out near the cottage because of the bears. In the morning, one of my uncles comes for coffee. He tells us about the moose tracks on the dirt road right behind our cottage. Then he leaves. He said all he had to say. I smell the bacon and eggs my aunt is making.

We will check the snares before we leave on Sunday around eleven. People say that when a hare gets caught, the pain makes it scream like a newborn baby. We rarely hear that. In the night, two or three miles from our sleep, the hare is caught and makes its last stand. It's better not to be there. People say it can make you want to give up hunting. ■

NOTICEBOARD

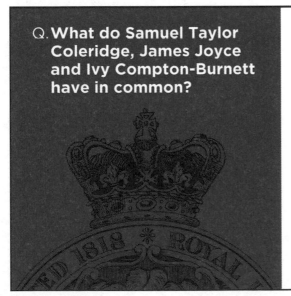

CONTRIBUTORS

Margaret Atwood is the author of more than fifty books of fiction, poetry and criticism.

Gary Barwin's novel *Yiddish for Pirates* won the 2017 Stephen Leacock Medal for Humour. His latest poetry collection is *No TV for Woodpeckers*.

Dionne Brand is a poet, novelist and essayist. Her writing has won several awards, including the 1997 Governor General's Literary Award for Poetry, the 1998 Trillium Book Award and the 2003 Pat Lowther Memorial Award.

Fanny Britt is a playwright, novelist and translator. Her first novel, *Les maisons* (*Hunting Houses*), was a finalist for the 2016 Prix littéraire France-Québec and the 2017 Prix littéraire des collégiens.

Daniel Canty is a writer and artist living in Montreal. He is the translator of poets such as Michael Ondaatje, Erin Mouré, Charles Simic and former Canadian Parliamentary Poet Laureate Fred Wah.

Douglas Coupland is a Canadian author and artist.

France Daigle is an Acadian author of eleven novels. She is the recipient of the 2012 Governor General's Literary Award for French Fiction.

Alain Farah was born in Montreal in 1979. His work includes *Pourquoi Bologne*, published in English as *Ravenscrag*. 'Life of the Father' is from his third novel *Mille secrets mille dangers*, forthcoming in 2019.

Sheila Fischman is the translator of nearly two hundred works of contemporary Québécois fiction. She is a member of the Order of Canada and a Chevalier de l'Ordre national du Québec.

Naomi Fontaine was born in Uashat, a native community on the St Lawrence River. She is currently pursuing a master's degree in literature at Université Laval and working on her second book.

Dominique Fortier's latest novel, *Au péril de la mer* (*The Island of Books*), won the 2016 Governor General's Literary Award for French Fiction. She spends her time between Montreal and Maine.

Krista Foss's debut novel *Smoke River* won the 2015 Hamilton Arts Council Literary Award for Fiction and was shortlisted for the 2014 Hammett Prize.

Kim Fu is the author of the poetry collection *How Festive the Ambulance* and the novel *For Today I Am a Boy*, which won the 2015 Edmund White Award for Debut Fiction.

Rawi Hage is a novelist and visual artist. His photographs been shown in Canada, Colombia, Lebanon and Japan.

David Homel is a literary translator and the author of eleven novels. His translations have won several prizes, including the Governor General's Literary Award for Translation in 1995 and 2001.

Anosh Irani's latest novel, *The Parcel*, was a finalist for the 2016 Governor General's Literary Award, and was longlisted for the 2017 DSC Prize for South Asian Literature. A longer version of 'Swimming Coach' is available on Granta.com.

Falen Johnson is Mohawk and Tuscarora from Six Nations. She is an actor, playwright and dramaturge. A full version of 'Two Indians' is available on Granta.com.

Benoit Jutras's poetry collection *Nous serons sans voix* won the 2002 Prix Émile-Nelligan.

Lazer Lederhendler is a translator based in Montreal specializing in contemporary Québécois fiction and non-fiction.

Alex Leslie is the author of the chapbook, *20 Objects for the New World*, a collection of stories, *People Who Disappear* and two collections of poetry, *The things I heard about you* and *Vancouver for Beginners*.

Alexander MacLeod's first book of stories, *Light Lifting*, won the 2011 Margaret and John Savage First Book Award and was a finalist for the 2011 Frank O'Connor International Short Story Award, the 2010 Scotiabank Giller Prize, and many others.

Daphne Marlatt emigrated to Canada from Penang, Malaysia, as a child in 1951. *Intertidal*, her collected poetry edited by Susan Holbrook, will be published in 2017.

Lisa Moore has written two collections of stories, *Degrees of Nakedness* and *Open*, and three novels, *Alligator*, *February* and *Caught*, as well as a stage play. She will publish a new collection of stories in 2018.

Rhonda Mullins won the 2015 Governor General's Literary Award for Translation for Jocelyne Saucier's *Twenty-One Cardinals*.

Nadim Roberts is a journalist from Vancouver whose work has been published in the *Walrus*, *Maisonneuve* and the *Globe and Mail*. A longer version of 'Mangilaluk's Highway' is available on Granta.com. It was completed at the Banff Centre's literary journalism residency, with the editorial support of Tim Falconer.

Armand Garnet Ruffo is a citizen of the Ojibwe Nation. His work includes *Introduction to Indigenous Literary Criticism in Canada*, *The Thunderbird Poems* and *Norval Morrisseau*, shortlisted for the 2015 Governor General's Literary Award for Creative Non-Fiction.

Chloé Savoie-Bernard was born and lives in Montreal. Her work has been nominated for the 2017 Prix littéraire des collégiens and the 2017 National Magazine Awards.

Anakana Schofield's debut novel *Malarky* won the 2013 Amazon.ca First Novel Award and the 2013 Debut-Litzer Prize for Fiction. Her second novel, *Martin John*, was shortlisted for the 2015 Scotiabank Giller Prize and the 2016 Goldsmiths Prize. 'Bina' is an excerpt from a forthcoming novel.

Paul Seesequasis is a Cree writer, editor, cultural activist and journalist. He was a founding editor of the award-winning *Aboriginal Voices* magazine, the recipient of a Maclean-Hunter journalism award, and a programme officer for a number of years at the Canada Council for the Arts. The photobook *Blanket Toss Under Midnight Sun* is forthcoming from Knopf Canada in 2018.

Johanna Skibsrud is the author of two novels, including *The Sentimentalists*, winner of the 2010 Scotiabank Giller Prize, one story collection and three collections of poetry. She is currently assistant professor of English literature at the University of Arizona. A new collection of stories, *Tiger Tiger*, is forthcoming in 2018.

Neil Smith is a novelist and translator. His novel *Boo* won the 2015 Hugh MacLennan Prize.

Karen Solie was born in Moose Jaw, Saskatchewan. Her third poetry collection, *Pigeon*, won the 2010 Griffin Poetry Prize. In 2015 she won the Latner Writers' Trust Poetry Prize.

Pablo Strauss grew up in Victoria, BC, and has lived in Quebec City for over a decade. His translations include four novels.

Souvankham Thammavongsa is the author of three books of poetry: *Small Arguments*, *Found* and *Light*. Her work has been shortlisted for the 2015 Commonwealth Short Story Prize.

Larry Tremblay is a writer, director, actor and Kathakali specialist. His works include *L'orangeraie* (*The Orange Grove*) and *L'impureté* (*The Impurity*).